Collecting
Fiesta, Lu-Ray
and Other Colorware

by
Mark Gonzalez

© 2000

Published by
L-W BOOK SALES
PO Box 69
Gas City, IN 46933

ISBN#: 0-89538-109-5

Published by: L-W Book Sales
              PO Box 69
              Gas City, IN 46933

Please write L-W Books for our FREE CATALOG of books on Antiques and Collectibles.

Table of Contents

Fiesta® is a registered trademark of the Homer Laughlin China Company

Dedication

This book is dedicated to:
Mom, Dad, Grandma, Aunt Opal
and
Agnes Boner, Florence Burris, Irene Deyarmon, Helen McKenna
Mary K. Swan, and my grandfather, Chester Tucker
along with every other potter who has ever shed blood,
sweat and tears for Homer Laughlin and Taylor Smith & Taylor.

Acknowledgments

This book could not have been completed without the information, pictures, opinions and advice from the following:

Steve Beals	Joe Zacharias	Steve Sfakis	Richard Racheter
Steven Levine	Ettie Newlands	Bill Mackall	William L. Smith III
Candy Fagerlin			F& C Stone

I would also like to express special thanks to those from the Homer Laughlin Company:

Johathan Parry	Joe Geisse	Judi Noble	Gordon Keiger
John Stoakes	Susie Bebout	Pat Shreve	

Introduction

Over one hundred and fifty lines of solid colored dinnerware have been produced in the United States from 1930 to the present day. Fiesta has become the most popular and most enduring of all these lines. Since it has been reissued in 1986 and continues to be produced today, many novice collectors and dealers have trouble telling the old from the new. So the first part of this book, the differences between old and new Fiesta (as well as other forms of Fiesta), is written for the novice collector and dealers.

Also covered in this book is another popular line of colorware: Lu-Ray Pastels by Taylor Smith & Taylor. Within the past five years or so the prices for this ware has skyrocketed. What some collectors may not realize is that there were other shapes made by TS & T in the Lu-Ray glazes. Some, like Conversation and Versatile, are rather easy to find and are more affordable than the standard Lu-Ray line.

Finally, various solid colored lines and items are shown to give the collector even more options. Some pieces in this book are being covered for the first time whereas others are being presented with a little more information and/or pictures than what is presently out there.

Prices in this book should be used as a guide. They are estimates compiled from various sources including collectors, and both real and online shops and auctions. Prices are for MINT condition items: no damage of any kind whether it be outside the factory or a factory flaw. Chips, cracks, crazing, kiln dirt, chiggers, flea bites, scratches, "glaze pops", etc. result in a piece not being in its best possible condition and prices should be adjusted accordingly.

There are some collectors who don't mind paying for damaged goods, but more often than not, AS-IS items just won't sell at any price. New collectors make the mistake of buying damaged pieces and then realize the mistake when they fail in reselling the item. Unless it is a very rare piece at a good price, or a one-of-a-kind, you would do better to spend your money on MINT condition dishes. You will see a greater return in the future.

I have been both a collector and a dealer and one thing I have learned is that dealers must be flexible with their prices. Collectors who see an over priced item (especially when damaged) with the words: FIRM are not going to purchase the piece and, consequently, the dealer is not going to make the sale. Everyone can relate to those pieces in his or her local antique shop that sit on the shelf month after month, year after year.

The main resources for the section on Fiesta are price lists that were issued by HLC and the modeling log. By collecting price lists, a general overview can be established as to when certain items and colors were discontinued and introduced. Many consider these to be the main source of information and have become collectibles themselves.

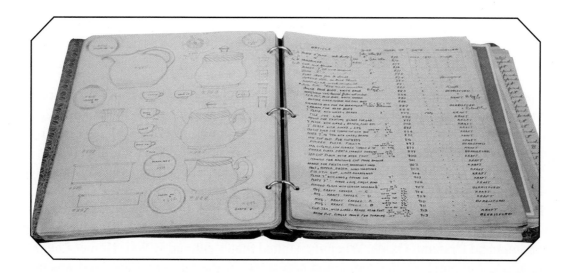

The modeling log is something that has been discovered by collectors only recently. There are several of these at the Homer Laughlin plant that have different ranges of years. The 1933-1944 log covers not only Fiesta but all the dinnerware lines introduced during that time such as Harlequin, Tango, Swing, Brittany, the Georgian lines, Nautilus, Oven Serve, Theme and Serenade. Some items were added to lines already existing such as Yellowstone and Century.

Information in the modeling log is presented in single rows starting with the "article" then followed by size, model number, date, and the modeler.

For example: the Fiesta medium teapot is listed as:
        TEAPOT, FIESTA 20 ozs 2covers   741   January 1937   Kraft

Many of the items from number 518 on have accompanying drawings of each item. Some items before 518 have small sketches in the margins. Also, the notation "released" was made beside an item when it was put into production.

The modeling log is best used to clear up some misconceptions on previously accepted dates and developments and many mold changes can be pin pointed with greater accuracy.

Old Fiesta was designed by Frederick Rhead and modeled by Kraft, Berrisford and Watkins. The development of new Fiesta is overseen by Jonathan Parry and the senior modeler is Joseph Geisse. In many instances in this book you will see the last names of the modelers, Kraft, Berrisford, Watkins and Geisse, associated with Fiesta pieces. They are responsible for giving form to Rhead's and Parry's designs.

The Various Types of Fiesta

Fiesta has been produced by Homer Laughlin (HLC) from 1936 until 1973 and reissued in 1986 and continues to be produced today. There have been several "spin-off" lines in the late 1960s and there is even Fiesta Mates, a companion line of New Fiesta. Collectors are left with SEVEN distinct groupings of Fiesta: old Fiesta, Fiesta Kitchen Kraft, Fiesta Ironstone, Sheffield Amberstone, Coventry Casualstone, new Fiesta and Fiesta Mates. One of the purposes of this book is to help the collector identify to which line his or her item belongs. First we begin by defining each Fiesta line.

Old Fiesta

The original Fiesta line, commonly called old Fiesta or Vintage Fiesta, consists of 67 standard items, 7 promotional items and has a total of 11 colors, which are divided into three groups: original colors: red, cobalt, yellow, light green, old ivory, and turquoise; 50s colors: gray, rose, chartreuse, forest green; and the last group consists of the rarest color: medium green.

The original 6 colors can be broken down even further. Red, cobalt, yellow, light green and ivory were the first to be offered in 1936. Turquoise came later in 1937.

Red (which is actually more orange than red) was the first color to be discontinued in 1943. Much has been written about this color and its radioactive nature. The red color glaze contains the compound Uranium Oxide. When the United States entered WWII, Homer Laughlin was no longer allowed to purchase the compound necessary for the mixture. Fiesta red was no longer offered until years after the war in 1959.

In the 1970s and early 80s, the myths about Fiesta red reached a peak. In some instances, people were throwing out (and in some cases burying) their red items afraid of the possible harmful effects. Today, no one really makes any commotion about this issue, and certainly no one is throwing out Fiesta red items! But, at one time, this was taken very seriously.

By 1951, ivory, light green and cobalt were replaced by rose, chartreuse, gray, and dark green. These would continue to be produced along with turquoise and yellow until 1959. These four replacement colors have become known as the 50s colors since they were made only in that decade.

In 1959 the 50s colors were discontinued but turquoise and yellow remained. Medium green was introduced and red made its return. These colors would last until 1969 when Fiesta was restyled into Fiesta Ironstone.

Fiesta Kitchen Kraft

Fiesta Kitchen Kraft (KK) is the second form of Fiesta. The items from this kitchen ware line were designed independently as a line all on its own. The KK items can be found with various decal treatments with an HLC backstamp.

In the late 30s and early 40s, various KK items were dipped in the Fiesta colors of red, cobalt, light green and yellow and sold as Fiesta Kitchen Kraft. All the pieces are of a heavy, durable body. In almost every case, there is a singular ring decoration around the rim.

Most of the Fiesta KK pieces are marked with the "in-the-mold" marking or a sticker. The cake plate, platter, pie plates, spoon, fork, and cake lifter don't have a mold marking and may or may not have a sticker.

Fiesta Kitchen Kraft assortment:
- lg., med., small mixing bowls
    - lg., med., Ind. casseroles
    - pie plate (2 sizes)

- spoon
- cake lifter
- lg., med., small covered jars
- covered jug (2 sizes)

- cake plate
- refrigerator stack set
- fork
- shakers

Fiesta Amberstone

The third form of Fiesta is Amberstone. Technically, this is a line of dinnerware all on its own and should not even have the Fiesta name attached to it. But many of the shapes used are from the original line and those that were created specifically for Amberstone were used in Ironstone and appear later in new Fiesta.

Fiesta Amberstone's *offical* name is "Sheffield Amberstone" and was sold as a promotional dinnerware line in grocery stores.

All the items come in a brown glaze and on flat items there is a black silk screen decoration. From the official order blank, the assortment of items includes:

- Dinner plate*
- coffee cup
- covered sugar
- large soup plate
- salad plate*
- sauce boat
- tea server
- jumbo salad bowl
- jumbo mug

- dessert dish
- saucer*
- creamer
- ashtray
- soup/cereal bowl
- relish tray*
- covered butter
- covered jam jar

- bread and butter*
- vegetable bowl
- oval platter 13"*
- shakers
- covered casserole
- coffee server
- round platter*
- serving pitcher

The jumbo mug is the coffee mug – not to be confused with the jumbo mug found in new Fiesta.

One item which did not appear on the order form but is on the cover drawing is the covered mustard. It is possible this item was under consideration to be part of the line but HLC changed their minds. At least one is known to exist, but I've not heard of any others.

Also in the cover drawing is a pair of ashtrays which look more like coasters and have only one cigarette rest. This was obviously not produced but the regular Fiesta ashtray was used in the line instead. The covered butter had a more rectangular design with rings instead of the version which was produced. Also the bowls had straight sides rather than the restyled flared type. Apparently the original concept for the jumbo salad bowl was the old Fiesta footed salad bowl.

The items marked with an asterisk are the ones which received a black decoration. All other items are found in a solid brown color. Since brown was not offered in old Fiesta and probably will never appear in the new line, Amberstone pieces blend in well especially the ones not restyled for this line. These pieces include: disc pitcher (called serving pitcher in the order form), sauce boat and shakers. The coffeepot and teapot are also the same as the older examples, except Amberstone items have a knob shaped finial.

Fiesta Casualstone

The promotion was repeated but this time antique gold was used instead of brown, and officially named, "Coventry Casualstone." The assortment of this fourth form of Fiesta is identical to Amerstone's though on the order blank soup plates, salad plates, cereal bowls and mugs had to be ordered in pairs. Prices were cheaper for many items: Amberstone jumbo salad bowls, coffee pots and teapots were $5.99 ea., but the Casualstone counterparts were $4.99 ea.

Casualstone's decoration was different from Amberstone's. It is more of a floral ring in brown as compared to the black stylized wreath found on Amberstone. Similar comments which were made on Amberstone can be made on Casualstone with respect to calling it Fiesta. It is up to the individual collector whether it should be included in his or her Fiesta collection.

Fiesta Ironstone

In 1969, the regular Fiesta line was restyled, making a fifth Fiesta incarnation, and named, "Fiesta Ironstone." The shapes used for Fiesta Ironstone were selected from the Amberstone line and came in three colors: turf green, antique gold and mango red (old Fiesta red).

The advertising pitch used for Ironstone was: "Color and shape come alive on Fiesta Ironstone to inspire a new contemporary feeling for today's casual indoor and outdoor living."

Items from Fiesta Ironstone include:

- cup
- 7" plate
- 13" oval platter
- cream
- shakers
- teapot*
- coffeepot*

- saucer
- soup/cereal
- vegetable
- sauceboat
- coffee mug
- 2qt. water jug (disc pitcher)*
- 10 1/4" salad bowl*

- 10" plate
- fruit (dessert) bowl
- covered sugar
- sauceboat stand
- covered casserole*

The items marked with an asterisk were, according to the order form dated July 1, 1969, "Sold in Antique Gold only" so don't expect to find these five items in turf green or red. Though, if you find the disc pitcher in red, it is from the original Fiesta line. The shakers were sold individually and not in pairs. Mixing and matching colors must not have been the style during this time since sets could be purchased in only one color. A service for 8 cost $41.55 in gold or turf green but $52.80 in mango red.

Turf green is a true 70s avocado green color. Individual prices for turf green were the same as gold but mango red as always priced higher.

Fiesta Ironstone was discontinued in 1973. No form of Fiesta was produced again until 1986 when it was reissued by Homer Laughlin.

New Fiesta first became available to the general public on February 28, 1986 at the Cultural Center shop at the State Museum of the Cultural Center in Charleston, West Virginia. First-day certificates were given to the buyers on that day and the Cultural Center sold it exclusively for a brief period of time until it was sold in Bloomingdale's and B. Altman's in New York.

The first five colors were black, white, rose, apricot, and cobalt. Old rose was a dark dusty pink color whereas new rose is a true bubble gum pink. New cobalt is a dark inky color that when viewed in poor lighting, looks almost black.

The original assortment of items in new Fiesta:

- Disk water pitcher	- juice disk pitcher	- sauce boat
- coffeepot*	- casserole*	- sugar/creamer/tray set
- pyramid candlestick	- medium vase	- teapot*
- shakers	- round platter	- creamer
- serving bowl	- covered sugar*	- round candlestick
- bud vase	- dinner plate	- 7" plate
- tea cup	- saucer	- soup/cereal bowl

The items marked with an asterisk were originally shapes from the Ironstone line. There were production problems and all of them had to be restyled.

In 1988 yellow was added. From 1988 until 1993, turquoise, periwinkle and seamist green were added as were the covered butter dish, 9" luncheon plate, coffee mug and the stacking cereal bowl. Several production changes occurred during this time; the finials on the individual and regular sugars became taller, the 9 1/2" platter was redesigned, the opening of the teapot base and its lid was modified and the rim inside the base of the casserole was eliminated.

In 1993, a lamp and clock were made as J.C. Penney exclusives. The lamp was made for only one season, and the clock was offered for that same time period but it was reintroduced in 1996 and has become a standard item.

The limited and now very desirable color lilac was made from 1993 to 1995. By this time the A.D. cup and saucers, deep plate, napkin rings, cake plate/serving tray, 12" rim soup, mini disk pitcher, and 13 1/2" oval platter, tumblers, pie plates and the utility trays, were in production. Persimmon followed in '95 and is a standard color today. Sapphire made a 180-day production run in 1996. Not only was this color limited by time, but not every item was made in sapphire.

The *official* items which were available in sapphire are:

- 10" plate	- 7" plate	- tea cup
- saucer	- 13" platter	- 6 7/8" bowl
- 39 oz. serving bowl	- disc pitcher*	- carafe
- tumbler**	- clock*	- handled serving tray***
- medium vase	- jumbo cup****	- jumbo saucer****

   *   comes plain or with 60th anniversary logo
  **   comes with new inkstamp or 60th anniversary inkstamp
 ***   comes plain or with FCoA (Fiesta Club of America) logo
****   Fiesta Mates

Some items that were offered for the first time in 1996 were: (these were never to have been made in lilac, but some do exist.)

- carafe	- hostess tray	- snack plate
- individual teapot		

Towards the end of 1997, apricot was discontinued entirely and black was placed on a limited status. Most of the larger accessory pieces are no longer available in this color and the simpler serving items such as plates and platters are made in limited quantities. Cobalt was to have had the same fate as apricot but demand has increased and this color is still part of the standard production.

Chartreuse, a Bloomingdale's exclusive, is limited and will end in 1999. Some items are made in limited quantity. Pearl gray, originally called Platinum gray, was released in 1998 and has become a stardard color. The newest items are the pedestal mug, pedestal bowl, tripod bowl and the 3-set mixing bowls.

Three vases, the Millennium I, II and III can be found in new Fiesta. The first one was made in ten colors with only 1000 examples in each color, however seconds were sold at the factory outlet. II and III will be made until the end of 1999.

Fiesta Mates

HLC has many general shapes which are used in the restaurant and hotel business which are often glazed in Fiesta colors and sold to various clients. HLC has dubbed this assortment of items, Fiesta Mates. These are NOT standard Fiesta items, but since they are done by HLC and in the same colors as new Fiesta, many collectors include them with their new Fiesta sets. Fiesta Mate items are utilitarian and have virtually no decoration.

Items available in Fiesta Mates:

- sugar caddie	- skillet	- colonial teapot
- oval baker	- ramekin	- Denver mug
- tower mug	- cream pitcher	- pasta bowl/rim soup
- shallow bowl	- Jung bowl	- jumbo bowl
- jumbo cup and saucer		

Here is the general HLC inkstamp. It is used on many of the Fiesta Mates and makes no reference to the pieces being related to Fiesta. Some items have an in-the-mold raised HLC logo similar to the backstamp.

Markings

Old Inkstamp

This is the only style of inkstamp used in the old standard Fiesta line. There are a few variations with the spacing of the letters in the words, "GENUINE", "HLCo" and "USA", but none are significant enough to warrant an excuciating analysis. It is important to remember that with <u>old inkstamps</u>, the letters in the word, "Fiesta" are all lower case.

New Inkstamp

This is one of three types of inkstamps found on NEW Fiesta. They all have one thing in common which differentiates them from the old stamp: the letters in the word, "Fiesta" are all capitalized.

If a Fiesta item has an inkstamp, telling whether it is old or new is automatic: OLD: "Fiesta" in lower case   NEW: "Fiesta" in upper case

Unfortunately, the same does not hold true for the cast indented markings, or "mold marks." There is no clean cut formula that applies to the different types of mold marks: some are found only on the old pieces, some are found only on the newer items and some are found on BOTH. Here is a breakdown of the ten types of mold markings found on Fiesta:

Mold Markings: Type I (Fiesta, HLC USA)

This marking can be found on almost every old piece that was cast. On this particular item, the water tumbler, there is a set of rings surrounding the marking. You will find this marking with and without rings. Pieces used in New Fiesta from the original molds (medium vase, bud vase, tripods) will have this marking.

Mold Markings: Type II (Fiesta, MADE IN USA, HLC)

Found mainly on small bowls (4 3/4" fruit, dessert bowls, individual salad bowls), this marking was used in old Fiesta only.

Mold Markings: Type III (HLC, Fiesta, MADE IN USA)

With the Type III marking, the HLC letters from the Type II marking are moved above the Fiesta logo. There are a few variations of this marking with the HLC and MADE IN USA being spaced close together, or far apart as shown.

Mold Markings: Type IV ([logo], Fiesta, MADE IN USA)

This is the same as Type III marking with the HLC letters replaced by the Homer Laughlin logo. Like the others, this can be found with and without surrounding rings. Type I and Type IV mold markings are the most common in old Fiesta. There are several new Fiesta items which have the Type IV mark since the same molds are being used. These include the disc pitcher, juice pitcher, sauceboat, individual creamer, individual sugar and teapot.

Type V through Type X markings are found on new Fiesta ONLY. Some may look very similar to their older counterparts. Here are the major difference between old and new marks:

1. OLD mold marks have the letters in the word, "Fiesta" running in a crisp, straight line.
2. NEW mold marks don't have the letters in the word, "Fiesta" running in a straight line; the letters are either uneven or in a circular pattern.

There are three exceptions to the second rule:

a. Type VII marking found mainly on the 13" platter and new utility tray
b. Any new piece which comes from an old mold.
c. 5 5/8" small bowl (found only in new Fiesta, it has a marking very similar to the old Type I)

NOTE: **Many new Fiesta items will have BOTH a new inkstamp and a mold mark.)**

Type V (HLC, Fiesta MADE IN USA)

This marking is found on several new pieces of Fiesta: new coffeepot, 6 7/8" cereal bowl. Here is a very good example of the letters of Fiesta not in a straight line. The mark is similar to the old Type III marking, but note the uneven positioning of the letters. Also the new "f" is not nearly as sleek and sharp as the older version.

Type VI (HLC, Fiesta, USA) - out of line

Same as the Type V marking with the MADE IN USA replaced by simply USA, this is found on platters, the butter dish, Tom & Jerry mug and teacups.

Type VII (HLC, Fiesta, USA) - in line

This is the exception of newly made markings in which the letters run in a straight line. Found mainly on the new utility (corn on the cob) tray and 13" platter, there should be no confusing this with older items. On the platter, the "f" is stylized to look almost like a capital "L": the only marking to have this look.

Type VIII (Fiesta, HLC, USA)

The newest trend in Fiesta markings is to have it run in a circular fashion. The "f" is still lower case and an "R" in a circle, declaring that Fiesta is a registered trademark, is added to all markings. The "f" may or may not be crossed at the top. Such is the case of the pedestal bowl which has a raised variation of this indented type. The presentation bowl, also in raised form, has the type VIII marking. Mixing bowls have an indented Type VIII mark.

Type IX (Fiesta, HLC, USA)

This marking is the same as they Type VIII variety, but now there is an upper case "F". This is one of the newest markings and is found on the 2-qt. bowl. A variation of this marking is found on the Millennium Vases.

Type X – New Carafe marking

Another mark with the upper case "F", Type X is only found on the new Carafe and in raised form.

There are 10 items in which telling the difference between old and new cannot be made by the markings alone. Some have been mentioned above, but here is a list of the 10 pieces found in both new and old Fiesta lines with their markings.

Disc pitcher - Type IV
Juice pitcher - Type IV
Medium Vase - Type I
Tripod/Pyramid Candleholders - Type I
Bulb/Round Candleholders - Type I
(variation that fits the underside)
Bud Vase - Type I and Type IV
8 1/2" nappy/ 39 1/4 oz Bowl - Type I & Type IV
Individual sugar - Type IV
Individual creamer - Type IV
Large Teapot - Type I and Type IV

For the above items, the mold marking is NOT a means in determining if your piece is old or new. In the past year, HLC has started marking these "problem" items with a small raised "H" near the mold mark. This is good for colors like chartreuse and gray which exist in both old and new Fiesta and were introduced in the new line when the "H" marking came into being. But keep in mind, these 10 items were produced for almost 12 years in new Fiesta without the "H" marking. The best way to tell the difference between these pieces is color.

If you are a beginner, then you will quickly learn to tell the difference between old and new by color alone for ANY piece without looking at the marking. However, at first, it may get a little tricky with certain colors like turquoise, gray and chartreuse – all three being found in both old and new Fiesta.

Type XI (Fiesta KK)

The Fiesta Kitchen Kraft mark is found on those items made in the late 30s and early 40s. Fiesta KK items may be marked with the special cast indented mark, or may come with a sticker.

Fiesta Colors

When considering all the various forms of Fiesta, there is a total of 29 colors. The majority of new colors are pastel in nature; old colors are rather bold-crayon type colors. Also, new colors have a very high glossy finish; old colors are rather dull in comparison. Here is a list of the colors from each form of Fiesta with approximate dates of production.

Old Fiesta		Fiesta Ironstone	New Fiesta	
red	(1936-1943, 1959-1972)	Antique Gold (1969-1976)*	white	(1986-)
cobalt	(1936-1951)	Turf Green (1969-1973)	black	(1986-)**
yellow	(1936-1969)		cobalt	(1986-)
light green	(1936-1951)		rose	(1986-)
ivory	(1936-1951)	Fiesta Amberstone	apricot	(1986-1997)
turquoise	(1937-1969)	amber (1967-1968)	yellow	(1988-)
gray	(1951-1959)		turquoise	(1988-)
dark green	(1951-1959)		periwinkle	(1989-)
rose	(1951-1959)		sea mist green	(1991-)
chartreuse	(1951-1959)		lilac	(1994-1995)
medium green	(1959-1969)		persimmon	(1995-)
			sapphire	(1996)***
			raspberry	(1997)****
			chartreuse	(1998-1999)
			pearl gray	(1999-)
			Juniper (soon to be released)	

* Antique Gold was also used with Fiesta Casualstone.

** Black has placed on a limited production status. Larger accessory pieces such as vases, candleholders, etc. are no longer available.

*** Not produced for the entire year.

**** Special color for the presentation bowl. For more, see section on same.

When talking about color availability on specific pieces, raspberry is not included.

One of the biggest problems with the colors concerns medium green. There are 7 greens in Fiesta and medium green is the rarest and consequently, the highest priced. The price difference can be staggering between medium green and other shades. For example, a medium green casserole can go for almost $1000.00 whereas light green examples fetch only $150.00.

Color comparison of the various Greens:

The shaker is in light green, the most common green of the old Fiesta line. To the left of the shaker is a teacup in dark or forest green – a 50s Fiesta color. Behind the dark green teacup is a new Fiesta chartreuse creamer. In the back is an old Fiesta chartreuse plate. New chartreuse has a "neon" quality to its glaze. The older chartreuse is darker in comparison and lacks the brightness of the new version. To the right of the shaker is a medium green teacup. Technically, it is an Ironstone teacup, but it has been glazed in the costly medium green. Behind the medium green teacup is a Fiesta Mate tower mug in Sea Mist green – a new Fiesta pastel shade. Finally, in the center is turf green Fiesta Ironstone bowl.

Blues of Fiesta:

On the far right is an old Fiesta teacup in turquoise. Behind it is a Fiesta jumbo mug in the new version of turquoise. New turquoise has a very slight green cast in certain light. In the back is an old Fiesta plate in cobalt. The new tumbler in front of the plate is in sapphire, the limited production run color. On the extreme left is a Fiesta Mate tower mug in new cobalt. It is the darkest of the blue glazes and is referred to as "inky" by most collectors. The little

ramekin sitting front and center is in a new glaze: a pastel shade called periwinkle.

Reds and Roses of Fiesta:

The bowl on the far left is in the old radioactive red. To the right is a tumbler in persimmon – a new glaze. Even though they may look identical in the picture, they are very distinct in person. Persimmon is a choral type red; the old Fiesta red is much closer to orange than red. The teacup on the far right is in the 50s color rose. It is a darker color, sometimes described as

being a "dusty" rose color. The shaker is a New Fiesta rose glaze. It's actually a true pink and found in new Fiesta only.

Ivory & Yellows of Fiesta:

The teacup on the far left is old ivory. In the center is a Fiesta Mate A.D. cup in new yellow. Many new collectors get these two confused. The old ivory glaze has a rich creamy look; new yellow is a glossy pastel shade. On the far right is a Fiesta Iron-

stone teacup in antique gold. In the back and on the left is a Fiesta Mate tower mug in the new (and now discontinued color) Apricot. To the right of the tower mug is an old Fiesta egg cup in yellow.

Whether it is in a major department store, an antiques shop, or flea market, pick up and study a piece of Fiesta. This talk of markings and colors may all seem intimidating at first, but in surprisingly very little time, you will be able to know the old from new on sight.

New Fiesta is made with a vitreous clay. This clay doesn't absorb moisture like the old semi-vitreous used in the old Fiesta line. Because of the differences in clay, the weights of old and new Fiesta pieces are different. In general, new Fiesta is much heavier than the old. To complicate things, however, some of the first new pieces from 1986 were made in semi-vitreous form and have the light weight feel of old Fiesta. These pieces are hard to come by today.

Fiesta Assortment of Items

In determining the difference between old and new Fiesta, we are going to start off with something very simple: the plates. There are several ways to tell old and new apart, but the fastest is to view the undersides:

Old plates: have a wet foot with three sagger pin marks. A wet foot means the underside is completely glazed. There should be no visible clay under the coloring. The pin marks always occur in threes and were used for supporting the piece in a sagger when it would be run through a kiln.

New Plates: have a dry foot ring. The dry foot ring is a rough, exposed ring of clay on the underside from sitting on a kiln shelf.

Another method is to inspect the ink stamps. Old Fiesta plates, especially those in the first six colors, may or may not be marked. When they are, however, they can be found with an older style inkstamp. New plates should always be marked and have one of the three versions of the new instamp. (For more on inkstamps, see section on markings.)

By this point there should be no doubt as to the age of the plate, but if so, new and old plates differ in actual diameters:

15"	old:	14 3/8"	new:	none available
13"	old:	12 1/8"	new:	11 3/4" (closest counterpart to old)
10"	old:	10 3/8"	new:	10 1/2"
9"	old:	9 3/8"	new:	9"
7"	old:	7 3/8"	new:	7 1/8"
6"	old:	6 1/4"	new:	6 1/8"

There is a plate coming out in new Fiesta as this book is being printed; the pizza tray. It measures 15" in diameter and is completely flat except for a rim around the edge. They will become a standard part of the new Fiesta line and should be available in chartreuse.

VALUES:

15" Chop Plate, produced from 1936 until the mid 1950s in 10 colors:

original six colors:

red, cobalt, ivory, light green:	$50-55
turquoise, yellow:	$40-45
50s colors:	$70-80

13" Chop Plate, produced from 1936 until 1969 in all eleven standard Fiesta colors as well as Casualstone and Amberstone. Reissued in 1986 is in production today (not including sapphire).

original six colors:

red, cobalt, ivory, light green:	$30-35
turquoise, yellow:	$25-30
50s colors:	$45-55
medium green:	$100+
Amberstone:	$30-35
Casualstone:	$20-25
Lilac (from new Fiesta):	$60+

10" Plate, produced in every form of Fiesta and available in every color.

original six colors:

red	$50-60
cobalt, ivory:	$40-50
light green, turquoise, yellow:	$35-45

50s colors:

chartreuse, gray, dark green:	$70-80
rose:	$50-60
medium green:	$125+
Amberstone/Casual/Ironstone:	$20-25
Lilac:	$35-40
Sapphire:	$30-35

9" Plate, much more common than the 10" size, produced from 1936 until 1969 and was added to the new Fiesta around 1993 (no sapphire).

original six colors except red:	$20-25
red and 50s colors:	$35-45
medium green:	$100+
lilac:	$50+

7" Plate, produced form 1936 until 1973. It has been part of the reissued Fiesta since 1986/

original six colors except red:	$10-15
red and 50s colors:	$20-25
medium green:	$50-75
Ironstone colors:	$5-10
Amberstone/Casualstone:	$10-15
Lilac:	$20-25
Sapphire:	$10-15

6" Plate: These were produced from 1936 until 1969 and can be found with Casualstone and Amberstone. They were added to the new Fiesta line around mid 1986 as a Stone & Thomas exclusive and became a standard item shortly thereafter (no sapphire). These are very easy to find in the first six original colors.

VALUES:

original colors except red:	$10
red and 50s colors:	$10-15
medium green:	$40+
Amberstone/Casualstone:	$5
Lilac:	$10-15

Here are the undersides of two old Fiesta plates. On top is one in old cobalt and underneath is an Antique Gold example from Fiesta Ironstone. Notice how the cobalt plate has two rings towards the rim. Casualstone and Ironstone plates (gold, turf green and red) will have a smooth area on its underside towards the rim.

The Fiesta cake plate in yellow is from Fiesta Kitchen Kraft. They come in red, light green, yellow and cobalt and are unmarked.

Values - any color: $45-55

There is a cake plate that was designed for the regular Fiesta line. They look very much like a 10" plate with the same type of ring configuration, but are completely flat. These are very rare and come in the first six colors only.

Values - any color: $600+

There is one design for the compartment (a.k.a. grill) plate but there are two different sizes. Shown in red is the larger size which measures 11⅝" in diameter. This was the first version and it was replaced by the scaled down 10½" size.

The large compartment plate is found in the original colors, save turquoise. It is generally accepted that the change in size occurred before turquoise was made an official Fiesta color in mid 1937. The large compartment plates are unmarked.

The smaller compartment plate, usually found with the old style inkstamp, was made until the mid 50s so don't expect to find them in medium green which wasn't a Fiesta color until 1959. Neither compartment plate has been reissued with the new line.

Values: 11⅝" compartment plate (commonly called the 12" compartment plate):
any color except turquoise: $60

turquoise: none known to exist

VALUES: 10½" compartment plate:
original 6 colors: $50-60
50s colors: $75+

These four multi-ringed plates could be considered Fiesta Mates. HLC made these in the glazes shown: persimmon, turquoise, sea mist and a washed out form of cobalt for the restaurant trade but they were supposedly rejected. Many have been sold through the seconds room at the HLC factory outlet. These have the general HLC inkstamp.

VALUES - any color: $15

There are three basic sizes of platters in new Fiesta: 13" shown in turquoise, 11" in persimmon, and 9" in turquoise. The 11" and 9" platters were added to the new line in mid 1986. The 13" platter came a few years later in late 1990. All three sizes are currently in production and can be found with an in-the-mold marking. All three sizes were made in lilac, but only one, the 13", was made in sapphire.

In old Fiesta, there is just one size, the 12½" platter. It was produced from 1937 and into Fiesta Ironstone so it comes in all the old colors as well as amber (with black stamp design), gold (with and without stamp design), and turf green.

Actual measurements of new platters:

13"	13½" by 9½"		9"	Two Styles:
11"	11½" by 8¾"			9⅜" by 6⅞"
				9⅝" by 6¾"

On the left in periwinkle is the new Fiesta 9" platter, actual measurement is: 9³/₈" by 6⁷/₈". These were introduced in 1986 as a Stone and Thomas exclusive and later became a standard item. They have a dry foot and a Type VI marking. This style is no longer in production and cannot be found in lilac, persimmon, sapphire, new chartreuse, and pearl gray.

On the right is the 9" replacement platter. Overall dimensions are 9⁵/₈" by 6³/₄". It has a much larger well than its predecessor and the rings are tightly spaced at the rim. These also have a Type VI mold marking and come in all new colors except sapphire.

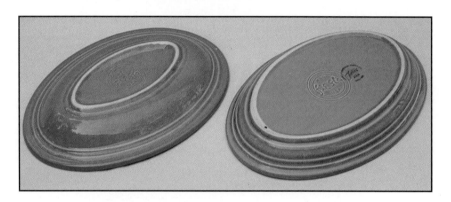

If you have trouble telling the difference between the two new 9" platters, measure the dry foot. Small welled (first version) 9" platters have dry feet that measure 5¹/₄" by 2¹/₂". Large welled (second version) 9" platters' dry feet are much larger at 7¹/₂" by 4³/₄".

VALUES: New Platters
      any size in lilac: $35-45
      13" in sapphire: $20-25

Old 12¹/₂" platters:
  red, 50s colors: $40-50
  turquoise, yellow, lt. green: $25
  cobalt, ivory: $35-40
  medium green: $150+

Amberstone, Casualstone & Ironstone: $20

The sauceboat stand was not produced in the standard line of Fiesta. It came much later in the 60s for Amberstone, Casualstone and Ironstone. As a result, they can be found in brown, gold, turf green and red.

These small platters measure 8⁷/₈" by 6¹/₂". Three rings can be found towards the rim of the sauce-boat stand; a departure from the standard set of rings normally found on Fiesta items. They are unmarked with wet feet and pin marks. Red is the most sought after since it blends in with the old Fiesta line.

> **VALUES:** red: $100+
> turf green and gold: $45
> brown: $30

The Fiesta Kitchen Kraft (KK) platters are rather nondescript. Measuring 12" across they are unmarked have a wet foot with pin marks and come in the standard KK colors: red, cobalt, yellow and light green.

Several have been found in Harlequin glazes including: Harlequin yellow, spruce green and mauve blue. These "Harlequin KK" platters are extremely rare. HLC records indicate that these platters were originally made for Royal Metal; a company that manufactured metal holders for platters and casseroles.

> **VALUES:** Fiesta colors: $70+
> Harlequin colors: $750+

These are new utility trays, commonly called, "corn on the cob trays." They have a raised variation of a Type VII come in all the new colors except sapphire.

> **VALUES:** lilac: $35-40

Here are two versions of old Fiesta utility trays (a.k.a. celery trays.)

This is the top view of the utility trays. Notice the "curved" sides of the cast example on the left.

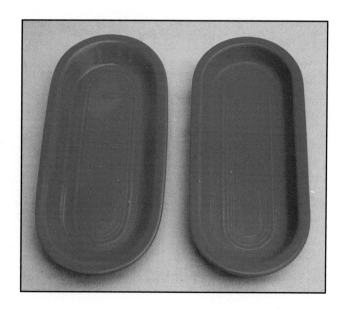

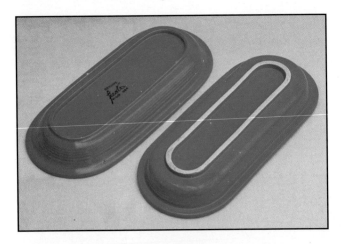

Cast on left, press on right. Press examples are unmarked.

Front view of utility trays. Again, cast style is on the left and press example with its straight sides and defined lip is on the right.

How did two versions of utility trays arise? Two different production methods were used. For the press, a ram press method was employed. This is basically a machine that forces a mass of clay to take on a specific shape. The cast style was made by casting which is a process that is familiar to many. A mold cast was made and wet clay or "slip" is poured in and allowed to slightly harden. The item is removed from the mold and is ready for the rest of manufacturing which includes backstamps, glazes, and heated in a kiln.

According to the modeling log, the wet foot version was modeled, for casting, on April of 1938 by Berrisford. Both styles come in the six original colors. They were discontinued around 1945.

Dimensions: Cast style: length: 10 7/16"   width: 4 15/16"
                Press style: length: 10 1/4"   width: 4 9/16"

VALUES: There doesn't seem to be any preference of one style over the other at this point.
any color: $40-50

This handled tray is from Fiesta Amberstone. It is basically the chop plate with a hole in the center with a metal handle. You will find corresponding handled trays in Casualstone.

Amberstone pie plates in their original packaging have coupons that can be redeemed for free handled trays.

VALUES: $20-25 - look at the handles to make sure the gold is intact and not flaking.

Both the snack tray and the hostess tray are part of new Fiesta and are marked with new type Fiesta inkstamp. These were being developed around the time of lilac in 1995 and were never officially made in that color. But, like the new carafe and Fiesta Mate Colonial teapot, lilac examples are known to exist.

Both of these trays are produced in all of the new Fiesta colors except sapphire and were never officially offered in lilac. Since apricot was discontinued at the end of 1997, and black has a special order status, prices for both trays in these colors should start to rise over the others.

The snack tray has a circular indentation which can accept a teacup or bouillon cup, depending if this is used as a "tennis set" or chip-n-dip.

The hostess tray, a design based on the handled serving tray, has a larger indentation than the snack tray and is commonly sold in stores with a new 5" straight sided fruit bowl.

The handled tray was introduced around 1990. There are two basic shapes as seen in the photo. On the left is the first style in seamist green. This comes in at least two versions which differ only in thickness. During production, cracks would form on the ends of the handles of the tray. To correct this, a continuous rim was made eliminating the various exposed partial ring ends of the handle.

The first version handled tray, which I refer to as "open" was produced in all new colors

except the most recent; chartreuse and pearl gray. The open tray can be found in lilac and sapphire with the Fiesta Club of America logo. Plain sapphire open trays were also produced as an HLC outlet exclusive. Only 1000 were produced and sold during the summer of 1997. Like all other limited new Fiesta items, make sure they come with the original box. In June of 1997, sapphire seconds were sold at the HLC warehouse sale. There were hundreds of open sapphire trays for sale making more than 1000 on the market. Unlike the "first quality" limited trays, the seconds were sold without boxes.

The second handled tray or "closed" tray cannot be found in sapphire or lilac since those colors were discontinued by the time the open tray was restyled into the closed version.

The first open trays made were rather thick and had a type VI mold mark. Thinner open trays and all closed trays have a new style Fiesta ink stamp.

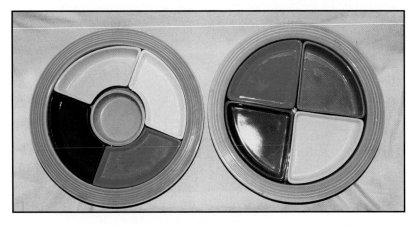

On the left is the Fiesta relish tray. It is made up of a base and five inserts. The tray on the right is from Fiesta's sister shape, Harlequin. Fiesta and Harlequin relish bases are similar in size but not in design. Fiesta bases commonly have a Type IV mark where as the Harlequin base, found only in turquoise, is unmarked. Also, Fiesta bases have the Fiesta style rings; Harlequin bases have the set of equidistant narrow rings.

The Fiesta base and compartments can be found in the first six colors only and have not been reissued. There are basically three types of relish sections:

1. flat bottom with Type 1 mold mark
2. flat bottom with inkstamp
3. tapered bottom with inkstamp

The sections with tapered undersides will be the thicker and taller than the other two. When mixing these sections, the resulting relish tray looks uneven. Flat bottom sections with inkstamps are generally the smallest.

VALUES: (for values on Harlequin relish, see section on Harlequin)
Fiesta Base: $65-75
Side section: $45-55
Center section: $55-65+

Undersides of relish inserts showing Type I mold marks. You will also find side and center inserts with tapered bases and with the old inkstamp.

This relish tray set is a dead ringer for Fiesta's right down to the tapered underside of the base. Each piece is marked: MAPLE WARE, MADE IN JAPAN with a maple leaf in the center. The pieces that make up this set are light weight compared to Fiesta and the colored glazes are obviously below standard since there is so much variation and runs.

Now, the question becomes: Which came first? Frederick Rhead designed both Fiesta and Harlequin and collectors of Harlequin know that Rhead copied Japanese imports with the basketweave style nut dishes and ashtrays so it is not at all unreasonable to assume he did the same with this relish tray.

The old figure-8's, shown here in turquoise, have a wet foot with three pin marks. The new trays, here in persimmon, have a completely dry foot. Also the markings are different: Old trays will have the old style Fiesta inkstamp and new trays will have an "in-the-mold" marking. Some new trays will have not only the mold marking but a new style Fiesta inkstamp as well.

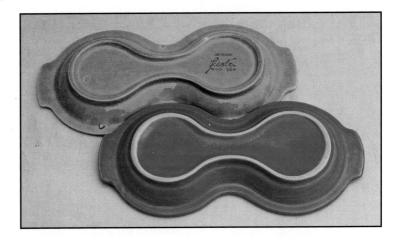

They also differ in size; old trays are 10³/8" long and new trays are a little smaller at 9⁷/8" in length.

Old figure-8 trays were part of a promotional set which included the individual creamer and sugar. The trays were cobalt and the sugar and creamer were in yellow. (see section on creamers and sugars for

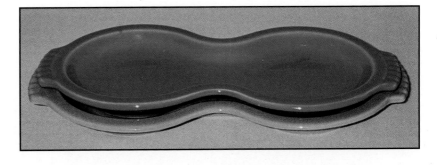

more.) A year ago I saw a vintage ad that had the figure-8 tray in turquoise with the sugar and creamer being from Harlequin. So far, those are the only two old colors in which the tray has been found.

It has always been accepted that the promotional items were released for sale in 1939. According to the modeling log, the fig-8 tray, cream and sugar set wasn't modeled until December of 1939 so these must have been available to the public AFTER 1939.

New figure-8 trays have been made since Fiesta was reissued in 1986. They can be found in all the new colors except sapphire. Here is a new tray, cream and sugar set in new chartreuse.

VALUES: old figure-8 trays
                      cobalt: $60+
                      turquoise: $200+
                  new figure-8 trays
                      lilac: $25+

Shown in red is one of the two sizes of pie plates from old Fiesta. These pie plates are from a general HLC Kitchen Kraft line and were dipped in four Fiesta colors; red, cobalt, Lt. green, and yellow, and sold as part of the Fiesta Kitchen Kraft line from the very late 30s until the mid 40s. The smaller measures 9¾" in diameter, the larger, which is the eaiser of the two to find, is 10¼" in diameter. All pie plates should be unmarked and have wet feet with pin marks.

Pie plates with Harlequin looking rings on the inner wall belong to Cronin's Zephyr kitchen-ware line. For more, see section on Zephyr by Cronin.

Here are the two sizes of Fiesta KK pie plates: to the right is the larger 10¼" size in yellow and to the left is the smaller pie plate with a diameter of 9¾".

VALUES:
  10¼" KK pie plate: any color: $50-60
  9¾" KK pie plate: any color: $60+

Measuring 9⅞" in diameter, the Amberstone pie plate is rather ordinary like the KK version except for the black silk screen decoration in the well. These were sold, along with other Amberstone items, as super market promotions. The pie plates had coupons that could be redeemed for the Amberstone handled serving tray.

Supposedly there is a corresponding pie plate for Casualstone, but I have yet to see one.
Amberstone pie plate: $30-35

This pie plate measures 10¼" and comes from new Fiesta and is available in all new colors except sapphire. These can be found with a dry foot (the only pie plate associated with Fiesta to have a dry foot) and a new style Fiesta ink stamp. The only decoration to this item is the double ring set on the outer wall as well as a crimped pie crust like edge.   New Fiesta lilac pie plate: $90+

Teacups from the old Fiesta line are found with a ring handle (shown in ivory along with Ironstone and new Fiesta cups for comparison.) There were several styles of handles under consideration including a version with the opening of the handle completely filled in. (For a picture

of various HLC handle and finial models, see photograph on last page of this book.)

The earliest teacups have a flat inside bottom similar to the early style sugar and A.D. cup. This was obviously changed very early since flat inside bottom teacups are hard to find.

The most common variations you will find with the old teacups involve the foot and interior rings. Examples produced prior to the early 1960s have a well defined small pedestal type base and rings running on the interior wall. All teacups produced after the early 60s have a blunt tapered foot with no inside rings. Since this change happened late,

old Fiesta cups without inside rings can be found only in red, medium green, yellow, and turquoise.

VALUES: (all with ring handle)

	cups:	saucers:
with flat inside bottom, any color:	$50+	$20+ *see next page
rounded inside bottom with inside rings:		
cobalt, ivory, light green:	$30-40	$5
yellow, turquoise:	$20-25	$5
red, 50s colors:	$50-60	$5-8
medium green:	$100+	$20+
rounded inside bottom without inside rings:		
red:	$40-50	see above
turquoise, yellow:	$20-25	see above
medium green:	$75-85	see above

For Fiesta Amberstone, Casualstone and Ironstone, the rounded inside bottom without rings teacup was modified by replacing the ring handle with a partial ring or "c" handle. Since Amberstone was produced concurrently with the standard Fiesta line in 1967, many of these "c" handle cups can be found in turquoise, yellow and medium green. Red ones can be found as well, but it is difficult in determining whether they belong to the standard Fiesta line or were part of Ironstone produced later.

VALUES:

	cups:	saucers:
turquoise, yellow, medium green:	$50+	see above
Amberstone/Casualstone/Ironstone (except red):	$10-12	$3
red:	$20-25	see above

The teacups used for new Fiesta are the "c" handled variety. These are marked Fiesta in-the-mold, but many times the glaze is so heavy, that many times the letters are unreadable. Sometimes when holding a new teacup in the right light at an angle, the cast indented Fiesta marking can be seen. Virtually all new Fiesta teacups will have a new style inkstamp.

New teacups come in all new colors including sapphire.

VALUES:

	cups:	saucers:
lilac:	$15-20	$5
sapphire:	$10-15	$5

Fiesta Saucers. On the surface, there is no way to tell the difference between these four saucers unless you know the colors.

Undersides of Fiesta saucers. Here we can spot the new saucer – the periwinkle example on the bottom right with the dry foot ring. Notice the others all have wet feet. They also have variations with the ring pattern.

cobalt: 4 center rings; 1 ring on the rim
ivory: 3 center rings; 1 ring on the rim
gray: 2 center rings, 1 ring on the rim
turf green: 2 center rings; 2 rings on rim

*   You will also find a saucer similar to the cobalt version but with a set of multiple rings on the opposite side of the raised foot. These are believed to go with the flat bottom type teacup.

The A.D. (after dinner) or demitasse cup and saucer were produced from 1936 until the mid 50s in all the standard old Fiesta colors except medium green.

The 50s colors: gray, rose, chartreuse, and dark green demi cups and saucers are hard to come by and will generally carry a high price tag.

VALUES:	Old Demitasse	saucers:
red:	$50+	$20+
cobalt, ivory:	$40-45	$15-20
lt. green, yellow, turquoise:	$30-35	$10-15
50s colors:	$400+	$100+

The earliest demi cups have a flat inside bottom. The rounded version was modeled in August of 1937, so turquoise flat bottom demis are the rarest.

The new Fiesta demitasse cups and saucers are found in all new colors except sapphire. Since the body of the cup was changed (handle remained the same as old), it is easy to tell the difference between the old and new versions.
Old: has a defined foot and interior rings and very rarely marked with a "HLC USA" inkstamp
New: has NO foot, NO interior rings and is marked Fiesta in the mold.

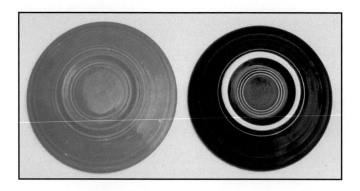

Here are the undersides of the old and new demitasse saucers each having distinctive features: (the same holds true for the regular saucer, plates, and platters.)

Old: may or may not have the old Fiesta inkstamp, has a wet foot with three pin marks

New: has a Fiesta inkstamp with a dry foot ring.

VALUES:

    lilac demi cup: $50

    lilac demi saucer: $10

The Fiesta Mate A.D. cup and saucer in yellow. The cup will have a raised HLC mark and the saucer will have the HLC inkstamp. Fiesta Mate A.D. saucers have a diameter of 4 7/8". The Mate cups stand 2 3/8" tall.

When looking at the standard old Fiesta line, Ironstone, and new Fiesta, you can find about two dozen distinct bowls. There are two dominate styles: straight sided and flared. Four of the straight sided bowls are from the original line: the 51/2" and 43/4" fruit bowls along with the 81/2" and 91/2" nappies. With new Fiesta, there are straight sided bowls that measure 55/8", 7", 81/4" and 105/8".

Sown in gray, this 43/4" fruit bowl is from the old Fiesta line; it has not been reissued. You will find them in all 11 standard colors and are believed to have been discontinued shortly after 1959 since medium green examples are incredibly hard to find. They are marked Fiesta in the mold with either Type I or Type II and can be found with both wet and dry feet.

VALUES:

    original colors: $25   50s colors: $35   medium green: $600+

This second straight sided bowl, shown in red, has a diameter of 51/2" and comes from the old line. It was produced for the entire run of old Fiesta and is found in all 11 colors. Unlike the smaller 43/4" size, it is not too difficult to find in medium green. Like the smaller 43/4" version, the 51/2" bowls will either have a Type I or Type II mold mark with either a dry or wet foot.

VALUES:

    original 6 colors: $30   50s colors: $50   medium green: $95+

The turquoise straight side bowl is 5⅝" across and is from new Fiesta. These have a dry foot and can be found in all new Fiesta colors except sapphire. They are officially listed as the 14¼ oz. Cereal Bowl and though this size is found only in new Fiesta, it has a Type I style mold mark. It is also used for the center of the 12" Hostess tray.

VALUES: Lilac: $40

The chartreuse 6⅞" bowl is another new Fiesta item. Listed as the 19oz. soup bowl, it is one of the standard items included in place settings. These can be found in all new colors with a Type V mold mark.

VALUES: Lilac: $30-35   Sapphire: $25

This is the original straight side Fiesta nappy shown in gray which has a diameter of 8½". They come in all eleven colors and are somewhat hard to find in good condition. This is not at all surprising since these make great serving bowls and were probably used quite often.

8½" nappies with either have a Type I or Type IV mold mark (sometimes in conjunction with an old style inkstamp) and will come in both wet and dry foot versions.

VALUES: original 6 colors: $45-55
           50s colors: $60-70
           medium green: $150+

The 8¼" nappy (not shown) is the new version of the older 8½" nappy. The official name for the 8¼" nappy is the 39 ¼ oz. Serving Bowl. This comes in all the new colors being easier to find in sapphire than lilac. All of these new serving bowls will have a dry foot and a new style Fiesta inkstamp. There may be some examples from 1986 which were made in semi-vitreous form which have an older mold marking.

VALUES: lilac: $55-65   Sapphire: $20-30

Another straight side bowl from the old Fiesta line: the 9½" nappy shown in cobalt. It has

been my experience that these are not the easiest serving bowls to find, yet demand seems to be low. They were made from 1936 until around 1945 so they come in the first six colors only.

VALUES: any color: $60+

This last version of the straight sided bowls is the newest one to be released. Modeled on February 5, 1997, these come in the new colors except sapphire, lilac and apricot. Shown in new chartreuse and measuring 10⅝" across, this monster of a serving bowl has a capacity of 2 quarts.

There are only five basic sizes of flared style Fiesta bowls. To begin, none were part of the original line and are not found in the old standard colors (except red which continued with Ironstone). The flared bowls were restyled versions of the original 5½" fruit and the 8½" nappy. A third bowl, the 6⅜" oatmeal, was added along with the restyled pair to be a part of the Amberstone, Casualstone and Ironstone lines. The two small flared bowls would eventually become part of the new Fiesta line.

Here is a comparison shot of the old and new oat-meal/cereal bowls. The turf green bowl on the right is the older example and comes from Fiesta Iron-stone. To the left is the new version in turquoise.

The undersides of the oatmeal/cereal bowls: the following holds true for all sizes of flared type bowls:

- OLD flared bowls are not marked in any way
- OLD flared bowls have wet feet with three sagger pin marks
- NEW flared bowls have a new style Fiesta inkstamp
- NEW flared bowls have a dry foot ring

VALUES: for OLD: red & turf green at high side: amber & gold at low range:
    Old, 5½": $5-10
    Old, 6⅜": $8-15
    Old, 8½": $20-35

VALUES: for NEW in lilac (neither size was made in sapphire)
    New, 5⅜"   lilac: $25+
    New, 6½"   lilac: $35+

Cream soups, with its lug handles indicating its all right to drink from the bowl, were made from 1936 until around 1959 or 1960. They have been found in all 11 standard Fiesta colors and are very rare in medium green so make sure you know your greens! All to often cream soups in light green are incorrectly labeled as medium green. The bowl part measures 5" across.

These are not produced in the new Fiesta line and come with various mold marks including Type I, Type III and Type IV.

VALUES:

red: $70-90

cobalt, ivory, light green: $45-55+

turquoise, yellow: $30-35

50s colors: $100+

medium green: $3000+

If you have a dessert bowl, then you have a piece of old Fiesta. They were made from 1936 until the very early 1960s and can be found in all 11 standard Fiesta colors.

You will also find them with both wet and dry feet. These shallow bowls are only 1" deep and have a diameter of 6 1/8" and will have either a Type I or Type II marking.

Medium green dessert bowls are very rare then followed by the 50s colors.

VALUES: red, cobalt: $50-60

ivory, light green: $45-50

yellow, turq.: $25-35

50s colors: $80+

medium green: $500+

These three stacking bowls were purchased at Homer Laughlin's Warehouse sale in June of 1998. The bowl is identical to the body of the HLC general shape number 114, the soup mug, except they lack the applied handle. All three, in colbalt, have the HLC in-the-mold raised logo. Measurements are: capacity: 13-oz.; diameter: 4 1/4" and height: 2 5/8".

Shown in seamist green and new turquoise, these little Fiesta Mates bowls stand 2 1/8" tall and have a diameter of 4 1/4". They can be found with the HLC logo in-the-mold raised marking. Called Jung bowls, they also come in persimmon and a muted cobalt glaze.

The ramekin is a Fiesta Mate available in only new Fiesta colors. Its official designation is Ameriwhite Product, item 0781, Ramekin, Milford shape. All ramekins have an in-the-mold, raised HLC logo.

Since apricot has been discontinued, prices have slowly begun to rise to $10-15 each.

Measuring 10" by 7 3/8" this oval baker in apricot is a Fiesta Mate. It can be found in many of the new Fiesta colors. These should have an HLC backstamp but I have seen several that were unmarked. This rather ordinary shape lacks any ornamentation and decoration.

Here in a clear glaze (not the applied color white) is a trial item that wasn't put into production: the Fiesta pedestal fruit bowl. It has an opening diameter of just under 6", and stands approx. 2 1/4" tall. Given the number of bowls available in the new Fiesta line, the addition of this bowl would have made it overkill. Still, this bowl's size would have made it much more useful than the stacking cereal or standard fruit bowl.

These are commonly referred to as deep plates. In general, new Fiesta items are smaller than their old counterparts, but this is not the case with the deep plate. When it was reissued, it was remodeled making the new version larger than the original.

To the left is the old Fiesta deep plate. These will have the old Fiesta style inkstamp and a wet foot with three pin marks. They come in all 11 colors as well as brown from Amberstone and gold from Casualstone. There was no deep plate with Ironstone and therefore is not available in turf green. Old deep plates have a diameter of 8³/₈".

VALUES: red, cobalt and 50s colors: $45-55   medium green: $85
ivory, light green: $40-45   brown: $10
turquoise, yellow: $30-35   gold: $25

The deep plate on the right is from New Fiesta and is officially called the 9" rim soup. These new pieces have a new Fiesta style inkstamp as well as a dry foot. They come in all the new colors except sapphire.   Lilac: $40

There are two other rim soups that are currently offered by HLC. The white one is part of the new Fiesta line: the 12" rim soup. There was no 12" rim soup with old Fiesta.

They come in all the new colors except sapphire and have a dry foot with a new style Fiesta inkstamp.   Lilac: $45

The other rim soup, shown in persimmon, measures 12³/₈" in diameter and is a Fiesta mate. These bowls, like other Fiesta mates, were not designed for Fiesta and lack the distinctive Fiesta ring pattern, but they can be found in Fiesta glazes. They have a general HLC inkstamp and a dry foot.

Found only in New Fiesta, and having a diameter of 9³/₄", the Pedestal bowl was modeled by Geisse on February 5, 1997. These cannot be found in sapphire or lilac. It has a raised variation of the Type VIII mold marking.

The individual salad bowl was a very late addition to the old Fiesta line. Introduced in 1959, these can be found only in red, turquoise, yellow, and medium green. Ordinarily, medium green would be the rarest color, but in this instance, each color is equally hard to find. For the most part, these bowls have an old type inkstamp but several are being found with the Type II mold marking. Then there are some that are not marked at all.

The yellow individual salad is identical to the green except in the following ways:
1. It is slightly thinner at the rim
2. There is no marking of any kind
3. There are no inside rings on the inner wall or the very bottom

To summarize there are at least three versions of the individual salad bowl:
1. with inside rings and a Type II mold mark
2. with inside rings and inkstamp
3. without inside rings and unmarked

VALUES: Any color, any variation: $85-95

This round shallow dish shown in sea mist is part of Fiesta Mates. It has a diameter of 7³/₈" and stands only 1¹/₂" tall. These are found with a dry foot and the HLC logo backstamp and do not come in lilac or sapphire.

The jumbo bowl a.k.a. chili bowl, shown here in new Turquoise, was originally part of Fiesta Mates. However, it along with the jumbo cup and saucer are rather popular and are quickly becoming standard items in the new Fiesta line. Still, expect to find a general HLC logo inkstamp for a marking.

VALUES: (not made in sapphire)
lilac: $30-35

The bouillon cups have a capacity of 6³/4 oz. They are new Fiesta pieces and are found in all the new colors except sapphire.

VALUES: lilac $35+

The little tripod bowl is a recent addition to the new Fiesta line. It doesn't come in lilac, sapphire, apricot, and will probably never be found in black since it has a limited status run. The tripod bowl is also sold as a candleholder. For more, see section on candlesticks.

This skillet is a Fiesta Mate and can be found in many of the new colors. It measures 11¹/2" by 8⁵/8". These are unmarked and have a completely dry underside.

This large footed salad bowl measures 11¹/4" in diameter. They are from the old Fiesta line and are found in the first six original colors only. They have a wet foot, three pin marks on the underside and are marked with an old Fiesta style inkstamp.

VALUES: any color $250+

This is the 11 3/4" fruit bowl in cobalt. This was originally designed for HLC's Kitchen Kraft: listed in the modeling log as: Salad Nappie, 11 1/4" x 3 (circa mid 1937). When it was decided to place this item in the regular Fiesta line, the familiar set of interior rings was added.

These can be found in the first six colors only since they were in production from 1937 until around 1945. This item is not found in new Fiesta. More than likely you will find them with a Type I mold mark.

VALUES: any color - $200+

This yellow bowl was offered as a promotional item in 1940. It was sold along with the Kitchen Kraft spoon and fork − all in yellow for $1.00. In Rhead's journals mention of this bowl was made on Dec. 26, 1939: "Releasing [model into production] Fiesta $1.00 special salad bowl model 1345. For Fiesta yellow only."

The promotional salad bowl has a variation of the Type II mold mark. They have a diameter of 9 1/2". Although these bowls were to have all been made in yellow, in very rare cases other colors will show up.

VALUES: yellow: $100-120   any other color: $1000+

Shown are five of the seven sizes of old Fiesta nested bowls. They are marked in the mold with a number indicating the size. All seven nested bowls were modeled in June and July of 1935 by Berrisford.

Sometimes it may be hard to read the number that is impressed in the bottom because of a heavy application of the glaze. This formula is commonly quoted on message boards online:

To determine the number of your nested bowl:

1. Measure the diameter of the bowl, outside rim to outside rim.
2. Round to the nearest whole inches
3. Subtract four
4. The result is the mixing bowl number

Example: Bowl measures 8.5" in diameter. Round up to 9". Subtracting 4 equals 5/ Therefore it is a #5 nested bowl.

VALUES:

	red/cobalt	ivory/turquoise/lt. green/yellow
#1	$250+	$200+
#2	$95-100	$85-95
#3	$110-125	$95-110
#4	$130-145	$100-120
#5	$150-165	$125-140
#6	$175-200	$140-165
#7	$250+	$200+

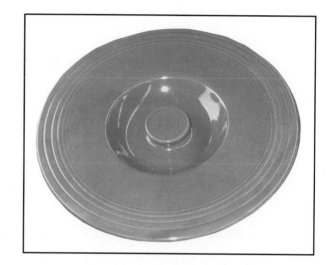

This is a #4 nested bowl lid. You will find a series of Fiesta like rings around the edge and on the recessed knob. Only four sizes of lids were ever officially offered with the nested bowls, but all seven were modeled in June of 1936 by Berrisford. A note written later beside the first four indicates they were released on July 27th, 1936. From this we can conclude the three larger sizes were mothballed, but a few #5 lids as well as a #6 lid has been unearthed. These larger lids generally bring thousands of dollars.

They were made for only a short period of time, and since I have never encountered any in turquoise, they may have been discontinued by mid 1937. When found, expect them to be in either red, cobalt, yellow, light green or ivory.

VALUES: Nested bowl lids – any color, size 1 thru 4: $800-1200

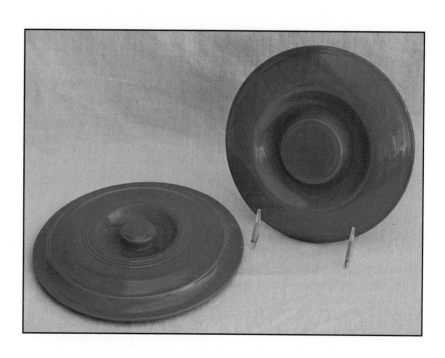

Here are two other HLC lids, both in red. On the right is the 8" Fiesta Kitchen Kraft lid and to the left is the Promotional Casserole lid. Because of their recessed knobs, they are often confused as being nested bowl lids and are worth considerably less.

Here are the new Fiesta mixing bowls in new cobalt. They are made to stack into one another but not flush like the old Fiesta nested bowls. These are rather recent additions so they cannot be found in lilac and sapphire. At the time of this writing, lids are being modeled for each bowl. They will have a gum drop like finial. Hopefully they will be released sometime around the year 2000, but anything could happen before then and the lids could end up shelved never having seen production.

The largest bowl measures 9¼" in diameter and is similar to the base of the casserole.

The medium bowl's diamter is 8½" and the smallest is 7½". All three have the same Type VIII marking.

HCL lists the capacities of these bowls as: small - 48 oz., medium - 64 oz., and large - 70 oz.

The Fiesta Kitchen Kraft mixing bowls come in red, cobalt, yellow and light green. From the largest to smallest, they measure 10", 8" and 6".

You will find unmarked mixing bowls in other HLC colors which were sold with other lines and really have no direct connection with Fiesta. Here are the other colors you can find KK mixing bowls in along with the appropriate lines:

medium (mauve) blue, Harlequin yellow - Harlequin
dark green, Harlequin yellow, chartreuse - Rhythm*
shell pink, celadon green, mist gray -   Jubilee**

* coupe shape line of dinnerware made by HLC in the 1950s. Colors included:
    maroon, gray, chartreuse, Harlequin yellow and dark green.
** HCL pastel glaze coupe shape dinnerware first made in 1948.

VALUES:		SIZES:	
color:	10"	8"	6"
red/cobalt	$125+	$90-100	$75-85
Lt. green & Fiesta yellow	$90-100	$75-85	$70-80
Harlequin yellow	$125+	$100+	---
Mist gray	$100-125	---	---
chartreuse	$175+	---	---
Celadon green	---	$90-100	---
medium (mauve) blue	---	$125+	---
Shell pink	---	---	$90-100
dark green	---	---	$125+

The jumbo salad bowl was offered with Ironstone, Casualstone and Amberstone. It comes in brown and gold only – they weren't made in either turf green or red even though those colors were available at the time, and measure 10".

VALUES: gold or amber: $35-40

Homer Laughlin wanted to have a special item made to celebrate the 500 millionth piece of Fiesta, thus the presentation bowl was born. It was modeled by Senior HLC modeler Joe Geisse on August 21st 1997. Only 500 were produced in the most limited color to date, raspberry. No other

Fiesta item exists in this ultra rare color and great efforts were made to keep it that way. Once the 500 bowls were produced in December of 1997, all the remaining seconds were destroyed and buried in a secret location within HLC grounds. The raspberry presentation bowls were given to upper management as well as upper echelons of their clients. The remaining were donated to various auctions. After being made in raspberry the presentation bowl was produced in all the different colors (except lilac, sapphire, and apricot) until the end of 1999.

Close up of underside of Raspberry presentation bowl. The raspberry color is a very dark maroon/burgundy. Each bowl is numbered and has a special gold marking along with a variation of the Type VIII mold mark which has a "500" over "M" signifying 500 million. The gold writing in the picture reads:

The Homer Laughlin China Company, Celebrating 500,000,000 pieces of Fiesta, No. 023 of 500, 1997, Newell West Virginia U.S.A.

Five of the raspberry presentation bowls were donated to the East Liverpool High School Alumni Association which auctioned off the bowls (also a set of exclusive chartreuse coffee pots were donated for this auction as well other limited items by surrounding potteries) on Sunday, June 14, 1998. With the proceeds going to their scholarship fund, all five bowls had final auction values that totalled $23,900.

Around the same time, another auction was held, this time the East Liverpool Pottery Collector's "Treasures of East Liverpool." One of the lucky winners was Peg Thompson who bought the bowl as a birthday present for her husband, John C. Thompson: CEO of Hall China. It's somewhat amusing that the head of the "competition" would pay big bucks for one of Homer Laughlin's most coveted pieces.

Each of the 500 bowls comes with a specially stamped box and a certificate of authenticity signed by the management of Homer Laughlin. When given the opportunity to purchase one of these bowls, DEMAND the box and certificate. Not only to be sure it is in fact the real thing, but because the box and certificate add to the value of the bowl.

Dimensions for the presentation bowl: diameter - 11 1/2", height - 2 3/8"

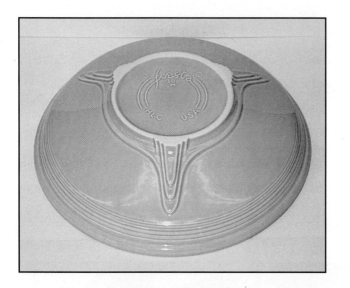

The underside of the presentation bowl has six feet. However, this was not the first design. The original model of the presentation bowl had three feet with each foot having three "steps" as shown. When the first batch of these were made in turquoise, a production flaw became apparent. The weight of the top of the bowl was too much for the three feet to hold. Thus, the bowl had to be modified.

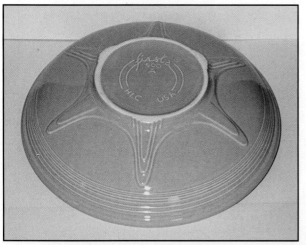

Here is the second version. Three more feet were added, but the additional feet only had two steps each. A batch of the second style was made in periwinkle and when the designers realized it worked, the added feet were remodeled with the extra step so all six feet would be identical resulting in the presentation bowl with which was released.

If you look at the underside of a presentation bowl, the three feet that extend inward forming part of the dry foot ring are from the original design. The three feet that are not part of the dry ring were the ones added later.

Some of the presentation bowls are made in mass quantities in the various colors of New Fiesta, however some have become limited. Black presentation bowls are sold at the HLC outlet only. They originally were to be limited in number, but that seems to have changed and now will be produced until the end of 1999. The Christmas presentation bowl is a limited item. They were produced for salaried employees of HLC and it is estimated that only around 200 were made making it more limited than the Raspberry presentation bowl. However, it is likely the raspberry will always be priced higher than its Christmas counterpart because of the uniqueness of its colored glaze.

The old Fiesta Tom & Jerry (T&J) mugs, on the right in red, are very simple in design: straight sided body with applied ring handle. These were produced from 1936 until 1969 and can be found in all 11 standard Fiesta colors. They stand 3" tall, have an opening diameter of 3" and vary in thickness. Most of the time these can be found with the old style inkstamp.

VALUES: Old T & J mugs: medium green $90 light green: $45-50
red, cobalt: $75-80 turquoise, yellow: $30
50s colors and ivory: $60

Shown in new chartreuse is the T&J from New Fiesta. It is similar to the old style T&J except the new version has a "fluted" opening as well as a set of rings around the top: old mugs have no sets of rings on the body.

New T&J mugs have an impressed marking, however, like the teacups, the applied glaze can be so heavy, the marking is usually "cloaked" by the color. Most of the time these can be found with a new Fiesta inkstamp, but because of the design of the opening, there should be no confusion between old and new. The dimensions for the new T&J mug are: height 3½" and opening diameter: 3⅝".

VALUES: Lilac: $25-30

This next mug comes from Fiesta Ironstone and Amberstone. It would be very easy to pass these by since there is nothing to the design that suggests it belongs to the Fiesta family. It can be found in the four colors of red, turf green, antique gold and amber.

VALUES: any color: $50-65

The new Fiesta mug in persimmon with a 60th anniversary logo. Other anniversary items include a disk pitcher set with tumblers, and clock.

This is the so called "Fan Mug" or "Horizon Mug." These are new Fiesta mugs with a special treatment. Basically a transfer decal-like film is placed over the mug. There is a substance in this film that reacts or "eats away" a layer of the glaze producing this impressed design of overlapping plates. These novelty mugs can be found in various new colors (no lilac or sapphire.)

Shown here in periwinkle, this is a special order mug for the International House of Pancakes. They can be found with and without the logo in periwinkle, rose and a clear glaze. The body is the Fiesta T&J mug and the handle comes from a 9oz. Shakespeare mug.

Supposedly, IHOP waitresses complained about the regular Fiesta T&J mug handles being too small. Thus, this variation was born. These have Fiesta marked in the mold, but since the glaze is usually applied heavily, it is not very easy to see.

VALUES: with IHOP logo: $10
without IHOP logo: $5

Shown here in new cobalt is the first version of the Pedestal or "Latte" mug modeled by Geisse on 4/14/98. It differs from the more familiar version by its beaded edge. Mr. Geisse explains that this first version would deform at the opening during the firing process. Instead of a consistent round opening, these pedestal mugs would warp due to the heavy rim. Only a few trial runs were made of this design in new cobalt and were never sold to the public.

The beaded edge mug was Re-modeled on 6/25/98 with a more flared rim, and released in late 1998, the pedestal mug comes in all of the new colors except for those discontinued by then: sapphire, lilac, and apricot. Pedestal mugs are a departure from the standard design of Fiesta. The familiar ring pattern is replaced by a quartet of "dancing" disc pitcher, coffee pot, teapot and vase. The measurements for these mugs are: height - 6", opening diameter - 4". They have a capacity of 16 oz. and a Type IX mold mark.

While the familiar pedestal mug was being remolded, a second design was considered. This mug was modeled on 6/3/98. Standing 6" tall, this "#2" pedestal mug in rose holds 18 oz. The style of the #2 pedestal mug is not as whimsical as the first. The coffee pots and vases on the side of this more cylindrical body seem to be in a police line up. A batch of these was made in rose solely as a trial run.

Shown with the #2 Pedestal mug is its mold. Notice the two little instruments in front of the mug; these are used in carving details in the plaster dummy models. In fact, many of the tools used on models in the art department at Homer Laughlin are make-shift employee inventions. The modelers use whatever they have at their disposal. Joe Giesse used something as common as a knitting needle to carve out the Fiesta logo on the new Carafe.

This mug in periwinkle was made specially for a friend of the Wells' (one of the families that owns HLC.) The story goes that Mr. Wells has a friend in England who doesn't like the small handles on various Fiesta items. So, this tall mug with a large handle was made. Again, like the beaded edge pedestal and the #2 pedestal, only a few of these were made and never offered to the public. These stand 6" tall.

The Denver mug, from Fiesta Mates, is hard to find in Lilac. They come with two versions of markings: one is the raised in-the-mold general HLC marking and the other is an HLC backstamp. The Denver mugs stand 3³/₄" tall and have an opening diameter of 2⁷/₈".

VALUE: Lilac Denver Mugs - $40

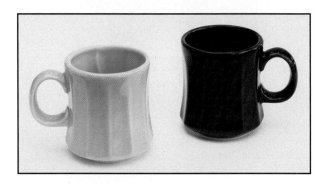

Also from Fiesta Mates, the tower mug is made up of 12 vertical panels. To the best of my knowledge, these were not produced in lilac or sapphire. They stand 3³/₈" tall and have an opening diameter of 3".

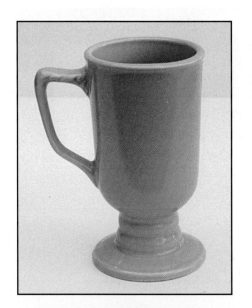

The Fiesta Mate Irish Coffee mug is another general HLC shape found in Fiesta glazes. Like the tower mug, this is not found in lilac or sapphire. Irish coffee mugs are generally unmarked. There are several potteries that produce Irish coffee mugs including Hall and Sterling China. The difference between HLC's and Hall's Irish coffee mugs lies in the handle. The Hall version is more angular and points upward. HLC's mug has the top part of the handle extending outward from the body and flat. Measurements for the Irish coffee mug are: height - 5¹/₂", opening diameter - 3¹/₈", base diameter - 3".

This last mug is also from the Fiesta Mates line. Called the Jumbo mug, or Jumbo cup, it holds 18oz. These mugs are identical to the Jumbo bowls, except the mug has an applied handle. There are many companies currently making jumbo style mugs such as Gibson. The Fiesta mates jumbo mugs have a very heavy body and are marked with the HLC backstamp. Unlike most other Fiesta mates, these mugs, along with the jumbo saucer, come in both sapphire and lilac. The jumbo cup and saucer have dry feet and the saucer is marked with the same HLC backstamp as the cup. Jumbo cup measurements: height - 3¹/₂", opening diameter - 4⁵/₈". Saucer diameter - 6³/₄".

VALUES:

mug: Sapphire: $15
Lilac: $20-25
saucer: Sapphire: $10
Lilac: $15-20

These are two mugs that were produced in 1986. Even though they have a Fiesta ring handle, the shapes are not Fiesta. They are HLC's general shape number 301 the York mug (8½ oz.) and will have the HLC Best China backstamp. York mugs are similar to other Fiesta mugs except they have a tapered bottom.

On the left is one of the mugs that was available at the Cultural Center at Charleston, West Viriginia which had an exhibit coinciding with the introduction of New Fiesta in 1986. The mug reads in red lettering: THE HOMER LAUGHLIN CHINA COMPANY: A FIESTA OF AMERICAN DINNERWARE, PRESENTED BY THE DEPARTMENT OF CULTURE AND HISTORY, THE CULTURAL CENTER, CHARLESTON, WV.

To the right is a 50th anniversary mug. The lettering is in cobalt, but they can be found with the lettering in all of the old colors except ivory. This mug reads: HLCo. FIESTA, FIESTA DINNERWARE, DESIGNED BY FREDERICK RHEAD, WAS INTRODUCED BY THE HOMER LAUGHLIN CHINA CO., IN 1936. The reverse of these mugs has the following in the form of a gold star sticker. COMMEMORATIVE LIMITED EDITION, FIESTA 50th ANNIVERSARY.

VALUES: either mug - $15

This particular "sit and sips" mug you see here was made in 1986 and has an HLC Best China backstamp. They were also made in the 50s and 60s with various promotional and advertisement decal treatments. These are not standard Fiesta items, but they do have the familiar Fiesta ring handle.

The regular sugar can be found in the standard 11 colors only. This version with scrolled handles was used only in the old Fiesta line, so don't expect to find it in new glazes.

Left: covered sugar
Right: covered onion soup

Many times the sugar is mistaken for the covered onion soup. Though similar in design, they are different sizes. The sugar has an opening diameter of 3 1/2" whereas the onion soups have an opening diameter of 4 7/16".

Onion soups were in production for a brief period of time (1936-1937) and are very rare in turquoise. Onion soup lids measure 4 3/4" across.

VALUES: covered onion soup:
original colors (except turquoise): $500-600
turquoise: $2000+

The earliest sugars have a flat inside bottom, a flared foot and a 1/4" thick flange on the lid. The oldest lids also extend out a little further than what is more commonly found. Sugars produced soon after Fiesta's introduction in 1936 have a rounded smooth bottom, a "stubby" foot, and a lid that does not extend to much further than the opening rim of the base.

These earliest sugars (flat bottom) have a Type I marking which is part of a deep underside; those that came later have a Type III mark with the underside filled in.

VALUES:

    med. green: $200+
    50s colors: $100
    red, cobalt: $75-85
    ivory, light green: $65-75
    turquoise, yellow: $50-60

Here are the old and new individual sugars which are part of the sugar/creamer/figure-8 tray set. To the left is the new version in black and to the right is the old one in yellow. Both have dry feet and are very similar in shape, but color is the key with this item.

Old individual sugars were made only in yellow, though only a couple are known to exist in old turquoise and both are without lids. New individual sugars come in all the new colors except sapphire. So unless your individual sugar is the old style yellow, it is 99.99% certain your sugar is new.

Notice the finial on the lid. In the early 90s, before lilac was introduced, the finial changed to a taller flutted version as shown in new chartreuse. The new Ind. sugar with a short finial can be found only in white, black, rose, apricot, turquoise, periwinkle, yellow, and seamist green.

VALUES of individual sugar with lid:
    Old - in yellow: $85-100
    New/short finial, seamist and periwinkle: $20
    New/short finial, other colors: $15-20
    New/tall finial, in lilac: $60-75

This is the brown Amberstone sugar. It is the same shape that can be found in antique gold from Casualstone, and gold, turf green and red from Ironstone. This restyled sugar is unhandled and the finial on the lid is knob-like rather than flared. Amberstone and Casualstone sugars can be found with both flat and rounded inside bottoms; Ironstone sugars have flat interiors. Unlike other items in Fiesta, none of the sugars can be found with interior rings.

VALUES: brown or gold: $20   turf green or red: $25-30

On the left is the Amberstone/shape sugar which was intended for new Fiesta. Due to production problems, the Ironstone sugar was discarded in favor of a sugar based on the old Fiesta marmalade. The old marmalade was redesigned with the notch on the lid filled in.

VALUE: Amberstone style sugar in
        new glazes: $100+

Just like the individual sugar, new Fiesta regular sugars can be found with small and tall finials. Lilac examples will have the tall finial.

VALUE: Lilac covered sugars: $80

Measuring 3½" by 2⅝" by 2⅜", the sugar packet holder shown in seamist green is from the New Fiesta line. These come in all new colors except sapphire and may or may not be marked with the new Fiesta backstamp

VALUE: Lilac sugar caddie: $35-45

This larger sugar caddie is not a standard piece of Fiesta but a general shape used by HLC. It can be found in various new Fiesta colors which makes part of Fiesta Mates. The dimensions for this item are 4⅞" x 2¾" x 2¼". Shown in periwinkle, it has a general HLC backstamp.

The stick handled creamer to the left is the original version. It was part of the 1936 assortment and continued until it was replaced by the ring handled style in late 1938. Even though they were produced for only a couple of years, they are not too hard to find. Since turquoise was introduced in 1937, stick handled creamers in that color are harder to find than the others which had at least a year head start. Stick creamers have a Type I mold mark.

This is what has become known as the regular creamer which replaced the stick handle version. The ring handle, given a designation of, "1104 for the body of the creamer" was modeled by Kraft in July of 1938 and was released the same month. Found in all 11 standard Fiesta colors, these continued in production until they were restyled with a partial ring or "c" handle for Amber/Casual/Ironstone. Ring handled creamers will have either a Type III or Type IV mold mark.

Neither the stick nor ring handled versions of the creamer are found in new Fiesta.

VALUES: Stick handled Creamer: turquoise - $80   red - $65
                                         colors other than turquoise and red - $50-60
                Ring handled Creamer: red - $45-55   cobalt, ivory, light green - $40-50
                                          turq., yellow - $25-35   50s colors - $50-60
                                          medium green - $85+

These two creamers have the partial ring or "c" handle. The creamer on the left can be found in brown from Amberstone, gold from both Casualstone and Ironstone and turf green and red, as shown, from Ironstone. These are all unmarked and very easy to find.

VALUES: Partial ring handled creamers: brown, gold - $15-20   red, turf green - $25-30

To the right is a new creamer in new chartreuse. It is the exact same design of the creamer used in the Fiesta "stone" lines of the late 60s. The new creamers are generally marked with an inkstamp, though I have seen many, especially seconds, that are unmarked. They come in all the new colors except sapphire.

New creamer in Lilac - $30

Shown with a turquoise figure-8 tray and yellow individual sugar is the individual creamer. They come in both old and new Fiesta, but with the old line, they were made as promotional items. All were to have been yellow, but as you can see from the picture, red Ind. creamers are found as well.

New individual creamers come in all the new colors except sapphire. Both old and new creamers are marked with a Type IV mark.

VALUES: old individual creamer: yellow - $55-65   red - $200+
new Ind. creamer: lilac - $20

The little cream pitcher is from Fiesta Mates. Shown in new turquoise and is a general HLC shape that can be found in various Fiesta colors. The company lists it as shape 0175, handled cream, jug, 5 1/4 oz. It stands 2 3/4" tall and the only marking is a raised HLC logo.

The sauceboat was not part of the original 1936 assortment but was added to the line in 1937 and comes in all 11 standard Fiesta colors. They have Type I and Type IV markings.

Sauceboats can be found in brown from Amberstone, gold from Casualstone and Ironstone, and turf green and red from Ironstone. None of the Amber-, Casual- or Ironstone sauceboats have any markings.

The new sauceboats, part of the new assortment from 1986 and currently in production, is taken directly form the old molds with Type IV markings. They come in all new colors except Sapphire. Because of the type of clay, they are slightly smaller and heavier than their old counterparts. Unfortunately, there was no remodeling for the new version which makes it difficult to tell the old from the new.

The newest of the new sauceboats will have the "H" marking along side the mold mark. Become familiar with the colors and weights and there should be no problem with other sauceboats.

VALUES: old sauceboats

red	$55-65	new sauceboats	
cobalt, ivory, light green	$45-55	lilac $50+	
turquoise, yellow	$25-30		
50s colors	$75-85		
medium green	$175+		

Amber/Casual/Ironstone sauceboats

brown, gold	$20-25
turf green	$30-40
unmarked red	see above

Shown in red the large teapot was made from 1936 until around 1945 so it comes in the six original colors only. They can be found with both Type I and Type IV mold markings.

VALUES: red - $275+
colors other than red - $225-250

The lilac teapot is part of new Fiesta. Note the dome shaped lid; old teapots have flat lids. This is the same lid that is found on the old Fiesta coffeepot. There are two major variations of new teapots: the first has a base identical to the old version with a large opening. This was modified with a smaller opening and the lid was remodeled to match.

VALUES: lilac - $85+

The medium teapot was modeled on January 1937 by Kraft. It is listed as: TEAPOT, FIESTA 20 oz., 2 covers. These two covers or lids are drawn off to the side of the item listing. Cover (a) is the lid everyone recognizes: round flat shape with a gum drop finial. Cover (b) has a flared finial that is similar to the lid for the large teapot but was never used on the medium size.

Shown in turquoise, they come in all 11 standard Fiesta colors and will have either a Type III or Type IV marking. The lid will generally have a steam hole but many are found without this feature in turquoise, yellow, red and medium green. It is believed that when many of the Fiesta shapes were being restyled for Amber-/Casual-/Ironstone, the medium teapot lid lost its vent and that these "holeless" lids are transitional pieces.

There is no medium teapot in new Fiesta.

VALUES: red - $250-300   cobalt, ivory & light green - $200-225
                yellow, turquoise - $150-175   50s colors - $350+
                medium green - $1500+

Shown in gold is the restyled version of the medium teapot which is part of Fiesta Amberstone, Casualstone and Ironstone. Even though it is an Ironstone item, don't expect to find them in red and turf green. According to the January 1969 and November 1970 price lists, the teapot, along with casserole, disk pitcher, coffeepot, and 10" salad bowl were never offered in any Ironstone color except antique gold. These gold teapots were listed as "Tea Server Covered" and were available for $3.60.

Brown examples come from Amberstone and are generally harder to find than the gold ones, which, by the way, can be considered Ironstone OR Casualstone.

The only major difference here from the original involves the finial which was changed from the gum drop shape to a more drawer pull knob type (though recently an unusual example in amber was found with the older gum drop type finial.) Other changes include the loss of the steam vent in the lid and the absence of a marking.

There is no Amberstone/Ironstone medium teapot in new Fiesta.

VALUES: gold - $45-50   brown - $35-40

This 2-cup individual teapot is part of New Fiesta. There is an experimental version from old Fiesta but it has a stick handle and only a few have been found in ivory. Shown in sea mist green, these little teapots were issued after lilac was discontinued. Not only can they not be found in lilac, they were never made in sapphire. Since apricot was discontinued only a few years after this teapot was introduced, and since black is becoming more and more limited, individual teapots in thos two colors should become more difficult to find as time goes on. The individual teapot is marked Fiesta in the mold.

The new Fiesta individual teapots will be part of a child's tea set that should be available before this book comes out.

This small teapot is called a "Colonial" teapot. It is not a standard item of the new Fiesta line, but rather is part of Fiesta mates. These were released shortly after lilac was discontinued. (Though they shouldn't exist, at least one lilac Colonial teapot is known.) In the future, these will be hardest to find in apricot (as shown) since that color was discontinued in 1997.

Here are the coffeepots found in old Fiesta. On the right is the original version in gray. It can be found in the first 10 colors (no medium green) with either a Type I or Type IV mold mark.

The brown coffeepot comes from Amberstone. These were also used in Casualstone and Ironstone and a commonly called "restyled" coffeepots. Like the medium teapot, this coffeepot differs from the old in that the finial is knob-shaped and its unmarked. Turf green and red "restyled" coffeepots were never to have been made.

VALUES: Original coffeepot:

red - $250+	turquoise, yellow - $150-170
cobalt/ivory - $200-230	50s colors - $350+
light green - $180-200	

Restyled coffeepot: amber, gold - $30-40

Shown with the amber "restyled" coffeepot is the new Fiesta coffeepot in lilac. Originally the restyled version from Ironstone was to have been used, but there were production problems which would cause the clay to warp and deform. The smaller coffeepot was put into production as a replacement.

New coffeepots have a Type V mold mark.

VALUES:

Ironstone coffeepot shape in new
rose, new cobalt, white, black or
apricot - $400+

New coffeepot shape in lilac - $95+

The stick handled A.D. or demitasse coffeepot is very popular with collectors. It is part of old Fiesta and comes in the first six colors only with a Type I mold mark.

VALUES:

red, turquoise - $600+
ivory, cobalt - $400+
light green, yellow - $300-350

The Fiesta Lamp is one of the more limited items of New Fiesta. It was made as a J.C. Penney exclusive in 1993. Shown in yellow, it stands 14¼" to the top of the socket. Even though this was made for less than a year, prices are somewhat low due to lack of demand. They have an estimated value of $85-125. Lilac, persimmon, sapphire, chartreuse and pearl gray were not in production until after 1993, so don't expect to find the lamp in these glazes.

The Fiesta Teapot lamp was modeled by Geisse on August 12, 1997. Shown in new Turquoise, this lamp is of the teapot with the lid and the base modeled into one piece. The top of the finial and the back have holes making it ready for wiring. These are not available in sapphire or lilac and were made for only a brief period of time.

To the left is the standard casserole in ivory. Part of the original assortment, it was produced from 1936 until Fiesta was restyled into Fiesta Ironstone. It can be found in 11 standard Fiesta colors with, of course, medium green being scarcest.

It is only one of three Fiesta items that can be found with the arch/scroll handles; the other two are the covered onion soup and regular sugar bowl. The regular style casserole is found only in old Fiesta – the casserole used in new Fiesta is dramatically different.

You will find interior ring variation with the base as well as type I and type II in-the-mold-markings. Also you may find bases of this casserole without the foot resulting in a flat tapered bottom base. These are marked "Tricoloator" and can be found in various HLC glazes. These Fiesta/Tricolor casseroles are listed in the Modeling log book as "CASSEROLE, PLAIN, SAME

AS FIESTA, 541/2 oz. CAP., [MOD No.] 1028, JAN 1938 [MODELER] KRAFT.

VALUES: red, cobalt, ivory - $200-250   medium green - $900+
                     light green, yellow, turquoise - $150-175   Tricolor bases, any color - $150-200
                     50s colors - $300-350

On the right in lilac is the casserole modeled for new Fiesta that is still in production today. Weighing in at 4.75 lb., it is one of the heaviest pieces of Fiesta. Gone from this version are the handles and the distinctive foot as well as the Art Deco/Streamline look that all preceding casseroles had. New casseroles can be found in all of the new colors except lilac. It was around 1993 when the new casserole's base lost the inner raised ring for the lid. Most recent casserole bases have a smooth interior. The base is used as part of a three piece mixing bowl set that is currently being offered by HLC. For the past several years odd bases could be purchased so don't be surprised to find these without a lid.

New Fiesta casseroles should be found with the new Fiesta ink stamps. Lilac examples (with original boxes) can go as high as $150+.

Dimensions: Base - height 33/4", base - diameter 51/2", opening diameter 93/8", lid diameter 91/4".

The French Casserole is one of the most unique designs of Fiesta. Its distinctive stick-handle and skillet-like appearance makes for a nice Fiesta prize. These were offered as a promotional item (one of several Fiesta promotional pieces) from 1940 until 1943. They were produced in yellow and sold for the whopping amount of $1.00. There have been a few lids, bases and complete sets found in non-standard colors, but if you come across a French casserole, expect it to be yellow AND from old Fiesta.

VALUES: base only - $100+   lid only - $150+   lid and base - $250+

This is a picture of a French casserole that is on display at HLC. Another was auctioned off on eBay. When the bidding ended on January 30, 1999, the final bid value was $8076.65 making it one of the most expensive pieces of old Fiesta. This ivory French casserole was the prototype and according to the modeling log, the modeler involved was Berrisford (who worked on many of HLC's casseroles) and the date is recorded as December 1939. It was later modified with the foot being eliminated which is the version that everyone knows as the French casserole in yellow.

Shown in red is a promotional casserole which was made for Royal Metal. It can be found in a wide array of HLC colors with red and light green being the most common. They were sold along with a Kitchen Kraft 9" pie plate as a promotional Fiesta set, again, like the French casserole, for $1.00. The bases are not marked and have a wet foot with three pin marks just under the rim of the bowl.

These lids have a recessed knob; not uncommon on some Fiesta items such as the nested bowl lids and the KK casserole lids. For some reason, lids are much more common than the bases. Don't expect this to be the case with lids of other Fiesta items. In general, lids are much harder to find than bases. The promotional casserole is the exception to this rule.

The bases have a pie crust design not found on any other HLC product. More than once I have encountered an uninformed dealer mistaking the base as a piece of Vistosa, a line by Taylor, Smith and Taylor which uses the pie crust motif.

VALUES: red, light green, cobalt
        base only - $40
        lid only - $40
        complete - $80 (note: many of these casseroles are found with base of one color and lid of another.)

Other colors
        base only - $60
        lid only - $60
        complete - $120

The casserole was one of the many items restyled for Fiesta Amberstone, Casualstone and Ironstone in the late 1960s. The finial became more knob-like, the applied arch/scroll handles became part of the base by being modeled into one piece, and the lid fits into the base rather than being extended over. These casseroles can be found in brown from Amberstone (as shown), and antique gold from Casualstone and Ironstone. Even though red and turf green were in production with gold in Ironstone, the casserole was made only in the gold glaze as was many of the larger items from that line.

VALUE: Restyled casserole: brown or gold - $50-75

When Fiesta was reintroduced in 1986, the casserole selected was from the restyled Ironstone line. The clay and manufacturing process had changed over the years and these new Ironstone casseroles came out of the kilns deformed. This phenomena occurred with anything requiring which was made up of a base and lid. A few restyled casseroles can be found in the new colors.

Here is an overhead shot of the three Fiesta Kitchen Kraft casseroles. The medium size on the left has an original Fiesta KK sticker. All have a Fiesta KK marking in the mold. The smallest casserole is listed as a bean pot in the modeling log.

All three casseroles are available in the four Fiesta KK colors: red, cobalt, light green and yellow.

VALUES: any color   large (8½") KK casserole - $100-125
medium (7½") KK casserole - $95-115
small (bean pot) KK casserole - $125-150

The Disc pitcher, shown in chartreuse, was originally modeled in March of 1938 by Berrisford. It would under go several modifications and eventually be included in the Fiesta line. These come in all 11 colors of old Fiesta, amber from Amberstone, gold from Casualstone and Ironstone (no turf green) and all the new Fiesta colors.

The old and new Fiesta disc pitchers all have a Type IV mold mark. Since the shape and the marking as the same for both eras, examine the color. Usually it is turquoise disc pitchers which cause the most confusion. The newest disc pitchers being made have a small raised "H" with the mold mark. If you see this mark, then the disc pitcher is definitely new.

But, new disc pitchers were produced for over a decade in the new glazes without the added "H" mark. I have both old and new disc pitchers in my collection and they all are basically the same when it comes to measurements. The old disc pitchers stand 7½" to the highest point. New versions stand slightly smaller at 7 3/16". Look at the inside of the pitcher where the top of the handle meets the body. If there is a pronounced indentation or dimple, then chances are it is new. The measurements on the bottom can be useful in deterring old from new. Measure across the glazed portion where the mold mark is (the area INSIDE the dry foot) Old disc pitchers should measure about 4⅝". New pitchers measure approximately 4⅜".

The best thing to do is become familiar with the colors of new Fiesta. Once you have done that, you should be able to tell the difference between old and new from several paces away without even picking up the piece!

New disc pitchers were sold with tumblers in sets commemorating the 60th anniversary of Fiesta. They came in persimmon, cobalt, sapphire, lilac, turquoise, periwinkle, rose, and white with a Tweety Bird decal treatment. The anniversary pitchers in solid colors have a 60th anniversary logo on the side and tumblers have a special backstamp.

J.C. Penney had an exclusive yellow disc pitcher with the dancing lady treatment in black.

VALUES: old disc pitchers: new disc pitchers:

old disc pitchers:
- red - $150+
- cobalt, ivory - $115-135
- light green, yellow - $95-125
- turquoise - $85-100
- 50s colors - $200-225
- medium green - 150+
- amber, gold - $30-40

new disc pitchers:
- lilac - $50+
- sapphire - $25-35
- rose-60th anniversary - $60-70

The old juice pitcher, 30oz., is found in yellow, red and gray. Yellow juice pitchers were part of a promotional juice set which included six juice tumblers. The gray juice pitcher was also used in a promotion which included dark green, chartreuse and Harlequin yellow tumblers. Like the large disc pitcher, new juice pitchers come directly from the old molds.

New juice pitchers, shown in periwinkle, come in all the new colors except sapphire. The only ones which should cause any problems are Pearl gray examples. Pearl gray is very similar to old gray, and with old gray Juice pitchers commanding $2000 or more, it is important to know how to tell the difference with these two colors. The markings are the same (Type IV) but new gray ones should have an "H" on the lower portion of the marking.

HLC is trying their best to mark the newest Fiesta items with this "H" marking and this should be your best clue in determining if your gray juice pitcher is new or old. A few new ones have been found in gray without the "H" mark.

Old juice pitchers:
- yellow - $45-50
- red - $250+
- gray - $2000+
- Harlequin yellow - $60+*
- Celadon green - $75+**

New juice pitchers:
- lilac - $65-85

   * Harlequin yellow is brighter than the yellow used in Fiesta
 ** Pastel green color used in HLC's Jubilee Line.

Celadon juice pitchers are part of a Jubilee promotion. Matching pastel tumblers can also be found.

This juice pitcher is one of the better look-alikes around. The design and dimensions are very similar and the color is a great match for the old Fiesta's yellow. The actual maker is unknown, but it has a mold marking: MADE IN CALIF.

Here is the Fiesta mini disk pitcher in cobalt along side a mini disk in light green from Sevilla Pottery line. There should be no trouble here since all of Sevilla's pitchers have a completely dry bottom and are unmarked.

The mini disk pitcher was added to Fiesta around 1993 the same time lilac was introduced. These cannot be found in the old line. It measures almost 31/4" to its highest point. All mini disks are marked in the mold.

These were not to have been made in sapphire, but I have heard of a batch of dozen having been made and leaving the factory. So don't be at all surprised to see sapphire mini disks in the future. HLC has tightened security in the past few years keeping the exclusive colors and limited run items from getting out of hand by employees.

VALUES: lilac mini disks - $50+

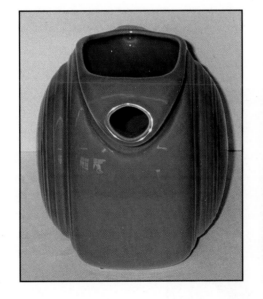

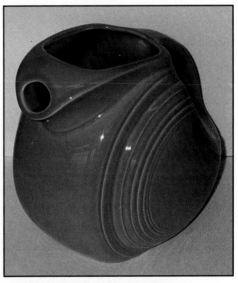

Here is one of the more unusual shapes created: the Anniversary Pitcher in persimmon. It almost looks like what you would get if the disk pitcher were crossed with a ball jug! These are identical to the standard water disk pitcher except for the extended sides. The in-the-mold marking is the same as the marking found on the regular disk pitcher except the HLC logo at the top of the word Fiesta is replaced by "60th." Having a width of 6" (compared to the regular disk pitcher's width of 4") it was intended to be a special item for the 60th anniversary of Fiesta. The powers that be rejected this item and it was subsequently mothballed.

It was decided instead to produce an anniversary set consisting of the standard disk pitcher with a set of tumblers celebrating Fiesta's 60th anniversary in 1996. Only the disk pitcher has the "60th Anniversary" treatment while the tumblers are specially marked with the Fiesta dancing lady.

The two pint jug, shown in gray, comes in the first ten colors (no medium green). There were actually five sizes produced. Like the nested bowls, each had a number along with the incised marking indicating its size. Two pint jugs are the largest and were designated number 5. On rare occasions, you may find one of these jugs with a "5" with the Fiesta marking. All five sizes were modeled on June of 1936, but only the 2 pint jug was released.

VALUES:

red - $80-100	lt. green & yellow, turquoise - $40-50
cobalt, ivory - $60-75	50s colors - $130+

The ice pitcher comes in the first six Fiesta colors with either a Type I or Type IV mold mark. It was part of the original line and was discontinued sometime around 1945. There is no ice pitcher in new Fiesta.

VALUES: red - $175+
        any other color - $130-150

This is the Fiesta Kitchen Kraft covered jug in cobalt. Its lid has a recessed knob like those found on the KK casseroles and KK covered jars. Two very similar yet distinct sizes have been found. They measure approximately 20" in circumference.

VALUES: any color - $225-250

Added to the line very early, the tumbler was discontinued by 1946. The light green one on the left stands 4 1/8" tall and has a Type I mark. The ivory one on the right stands approximately 4" and has a Type IV marking. Though I can find no record of this apparent change in mold, it probably happened early since the shorter tumblers are much more common than the slightly larger counterparts. The larger version will hold a full fluid ounce more than the standard 10oz. tumbler.

Like all tumblers shown in the model log, the Fiesta tumbler is referred to as a "mug." There were two styles designed; shape number 735 listed as a Fiesta mug, convex was modeled by Kraft in December of 1936. Shape number 736, Fiesta mug, concave, was modeled by Berrisford again, in December '36. Interestingly Kraft's was not released. This is somewhat unusual since he was the primary modeler of Fiesta. The tumbler or "mug" that collectors are familiar with is Berrisford's shape number 736, the concave mug.

VALUES: red - $85   light green, turquoise, yellow - $50-60
                cobalt, ivory - $65-75

HLC's Harlequin line also had a water tumbler. Shown on the right in rose, it is smaller than Fiesta's shown on the left in light green. Every Fiesta water tumbler will be marked as opposed to Harlequin's which are never marked.

Shown on the right are the old Fiesta juice tumblers. There's well over a dozen mentions of the juice tumbler in the modeling log in the form of "Kraft cheese jars." Apparently HLC worked with Kraft Cheese in making a swanky swig-like container for Kraft products. For some reason, they just couldn't seem to get it right! Variations were made to the diameter of the opening height and overall shape.

These containers would eventually become Fiesta juice tumblers and sold, along with the Fiesta juice pitcher in yellow, as promotional items. The promotion was also used in Jubilee and Rhythm, so there is a wide array of colors available for the old Fiesta juice tumblers.

VALUES:

red, cobalt, ivory - $35-45   chartreuse, Harlequin, yellow & dk. green - $500+**
lt. green, yellow, turquoise - $20-25 mist gray - $225+***
rose - $50-55*   Shell pink, cream beige - $95-110***

   * Rose juice tumblers are not uncommon. Some collectors hold to the old notion that this was "borrowed" to add a seventh color to the juice set. Others think it is more likely that it was a replacement color for red when it was discontinued in 1943.

  ** These tumblers are from the Rhythm colored juice set. They were sold with the gray juice pitcher.

*** These tumblers are from the Jubilee juice set - a pastel dinnerware line first made by HLC in 1948. Gray should be as common as Shell Pink and Cream Beige, but since the Mist gray color blends in with the rest of Fiesta, collectors are willing to pay more for gray juice tumblers.

To the right of the old Fiesta examples are new Fiesta tumblers in black, sapphire and periwinkle. They are taller and wider than the older versions (3$\frac{3}{4}$" tall, 2$\frac{15}{16}$" opening diameter). Originally, these were made as part of the 60th anniversary sets but were added as permanent items to the new Fiesta line.

You will find two distinct markings: the new style Fiesta inkstamp and the 60th anniversary inkstamp which also has a dancing lady. Rose anniversary sets were rather limited in number and, as a result, the pitchers and tumblers have gone up in price.

VALUES: New Fiesta tumblers: specially marked 60th anniversary tumblers
        any color except rose - $15
        rose - $30+

new Fiesta marking tumblers
        lilac - $15-20
        sapphire - $10-15

The Fiesta juice tumbler is shown in ivory. Beside it, in green is a Sevilla juice tumbler made by The Cronin China Company. The Sevilla tumblers are rather common and are almost always mistaken for Fiesta. See section on Sevilla for more.

This look-alike juice tumbler was found in a California shop. Its dimensions are: diameter 2$\frac{1}{2}$"; height 3$\frac{1}{4}$"; base diameter 1$\frac{15}{16}$". The glaze is a rather uncommon dark orange/tomato color and it has a pronounced flare to the opening.

This is a case where the old style was restyled dramatically, resulting in very different shapes. On the left is the old Fiesta carafe in ivory and on the right is the new version in turquoise. There are four major differences between the old and new carafes.

1. The first and most obvious is the lid. Old carafes have a lid which has a cork seal. New carafes have no lids

2. The second difference is ring placement. The old style has a set of rings on its foot and the underside of its opening. New carafes have rings just under the neck and none under the opening.

3. The third difference is in regard to the base. Old carafes have a distinctive foot whereas the new carafe has a short tapered bottom.

4. Finally, they each have dissimilar markings. The old carafe has an indented mold marking: Types I and IV. The new Carafe has a raised marking: Type X.

Because of their shapes, carafes, both old and new, are very popular. Old carafes come in the first six colors only and was produced from the beginning in 1936 and was discontinued by 1946. The new carafe is a late addition to the new line being put into production shortly after lilac was retired in 1995. Though none *should* ever be found on the market, a batch of carafes were produced in lilac as a test run. At least one of these can be seen in the HLC museum at the outlet.

Old carafes are actually not very hard to find. When cleaning the lid, try not to get the cork part wet. These will expand and make a difficult fit on the base. (I found out the hard way!)

Although you may not find lilac carafes, they are available in every other new color. Given that apricot was recently discontinued and black has been cut way back, those are the two colors to watch since carafes in those colors were produced for only five years. Sapphire carafes are not at all uncommon, but were made for only its 180-day run.

VALUES: Old Fiesta Carafes
                    red, cobalt, ivory - $250+   light green, yellow and turquoise - $175-225
           New Carafes in sapphire - $45+

There were two sizes of comports modeled for Fiesta, but only one went into production. The first was modeled in April of 1935. It measures 10" in diameter and stands 2¹/₂" tall. The second version, which has a diameter of 12" and stands 3¹/₄", is the one that became a standard item. Both were modeled by Berrisford.

Shown in red, the 12" comport is marked with an old style Fiesta inkstamp. These were discontinued around 1945 so they come in the first six colors only. They have not been reissued with new Fiesta.

VALUES: 12" comport
                red - $200+
                cobalt, ivory - $145-170
                lt. green, yellow, turquoise - $100-125

The sweets compote or just compote was made from 1936 until around 1945. It comes in the first six colors only and is not being produced in new Fiesta. Some may be marked with "HLC USA." Many collectors seem to think that this marking was used on normally unmarked Fiesta such as the compotes, teacups, demi cups, shakers and covered mustards that was exported to Canada.

VALUES: sweets compote

    red, cobalt, ivory - $100+

    turq., lt. green, yellow - $75-95

The tripod candleholders are one of the more popular shapes in Fiesta. They were part of the old line from 1936 until 1942 and come in the first six colors only. Called pyramid candlesticks, they were part of the reissue in 1986 and continue to be produced today. Tripods found in both eras have the same Type I marking.

Old tripods are worth considerably more than their new counterparts, and there is a simple way to tell the difference: the old tripods will have a wet foot with three pin marks; new tripods have a dry foot. There are only one or two pairs of old tripods which are found to have a dry foot and these are believed to be the earliest produced.

Notice the "H" at the bottom on the new tripod. This mark has recently been added to many new Fiesta shapes which will aid collectors in telling the old from the new. Keep in mind that new Fiesta was produced for over 10 years without this "H" marking.

New tripods in lilac were made in limited quantity as Bloomingdales exclusives and have soared in price rivaling the older colors.

Considering they are not found often in mint condition, they must have broken easily. Watch for small chips and repairs on the undersides of the "steps" on these items.

VALUES: (prices given are for a PAIR)

    old tripods - original six colors, any color - $700+

    new tripods - lilac - $500

You will find the bulb type candleholders in both old and new Fiesta. They were modeled on September of 1935 by Watkins and are listed as: CANDLESTICK, SQUARE BASE. According to the log several candleholders were modeled around the same time. (There is one earlier version which looks like the standard ball shape with the familiar pedestal foot making it look similar to the marmalade. Tiny scroll-like handles towards the top complete the look.)

The molds used in both old and new Fiesta are identical, so markings won't help in determining the difference. Also, both have dry feet. But, because of the different clays used today as compared to when old Fiesta was manufactured, the heights will be different.

OLD: base measurement of each square side - 2⁷/16", height 3³/4"

NEW: base measurement of each square side - 2³/8", height 3¹/2"

Old bulb candleholders were made in the first six colors of old Fiesta: red, cobalt, light green, yellow, turquoise, and old ivory. They can be found in all the new Fiesta colors except sapphire. Unlike the tripod style, bulb type candleholders are common.

VALUES: (prices given are for a PAIR)
    old colors: red, cobalt - $100-115
          ivory, turquoise, yellow & light green - $75-85
    new colors: lilac - $75+

This pair of look-alike bulb candleholders in cobalt were made by Paden City Pottery for their line, Caliente. These are unmarked and lack any ring design.

Here is the little tripod bowl from new Fiesta acting as a votive. These are sold complete with candle and box.

left: Casualstone Marmalade in gold, old Fiesta Marmalade in light green.

Originally called a "Covered Honey" in the modeling log, the covered marmalade, on the right in light green, was made from late 1936 until around 1945 and come in the first six colors only. Look for damage around the notch opening on the lid. These generally have a Type I mold mark.

To the left is the Casualstone marmalade which was produced in the late 1960s. There is a corresponding one in brown from the Amberstone line. These are unmarked and the only difference in shape is with the lid. The Casual/Amberstone lids have a knob like finial compared to the old flared style.

The marmalade base was used for the new Fiesta sugar when it was realized the Ironstone sugar wouldn't work. The most obvious difference between an old marmalade and a new sugar is the lid; new sugar lids do not have the cut out notch for a spoon.

Shown with the marmalade is the little covered mustard jar in turquoise. These are generally unmarked, but some can be found with the HLC USA marking. They differ from their larger counterpart in that the mustard has a gum drop shape finial.

VALUES:
 either covd mustard or covd marmalade:
  red, cobalt, ivory & turquoise - $255+
  lt. green, yellow - $180-200
  covd marmalade in gold or amber - $45-55

A comparison photo showing the similarity in size of a red mustard with a light green shaker.

68

Napkin rings are found in new Fiesta only. They were modeled in late 1991 and were soon added to the new Fiesta line. There are no sapphire napkin rings, but they can be found in every other new color.

VALUE: Lilac napkin ring
(single) - $25-30

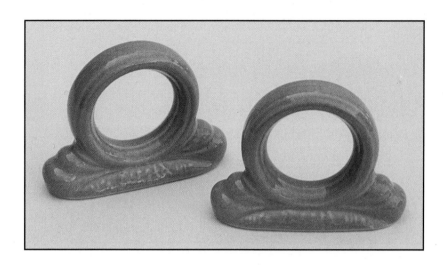

The small light green shaker can be found in all 11 colors of old Fiesta, brown from Amberstone, gold from Casualstone and Ironstone, turf green (and red) from Ironstone and all the new colors, except sapphire. The larger shaker in red is from Fiesta Kitchen Kraft.

The old pairs had the holes in different sizes to differentiate the salt from the pepper. Towards the late 60s, the center hole in one was eliminated thus salt and pepper could be designated by the number of holes. The 6/7 hole shakers were used primarily in Amberstone, Casualstone and Ironstone, but several pairs have been found in turquoise, yellow and medium green. (Red examples would belong to Ironstone.)

New Fiesta shakers use the 6/7 hole configuration and are sold with plastic or rubber stoppers (old shakers will generally be found with cork stoppers.) Once in a while, an old shaker will turn up with an HLC USA marking. All new shakers are unmarked. White new shakers with red trim belong to a line of Christmas Fiesta.

VALUES: shakers in PAIRS
old shakers
red - $35-40   med. green - $85-100
cobalt, ivory - $25-35   amber, gold - $10-15
lt. green, turq., yellow - $20-25   turf green - $20-25
50s colors - $35-40

new shakers in lilac - $55+

Here are the Fiesta Kitchen Kraft shakers in the four KK colors: red, yellow, light green and cobalt. As with the older and smaller regular Fiesta shakers, the KK versions all have seven holes with different sizes to tell the salt from the pepper.

Fiesta shakers are unmarked.

VALUES: a pair, any color - $85-95

The range shakers are from new Fiesta and are rather recent additions. They come in all the new colors except sapphire and lilac. The holes are arranged in the letters "S" and "P" to denote which is salt and which is pepper. These are marked in the mold in a circular fashion and are sold with rubber stoppers.

There was never a Fiesta butter dish in the old Fiesta assortment. It seems strange that a line could be produced with such an array of accessories such as mustards, marmalades, relish trays, vases, etc. yet not include a butter dish. There are however, butter dishes offered in Fiesta's sister lines: Harlequin and Riviera.

This stick butter dish was produced in antique gold for Fiesta Casualstone in 1968 and brown for Fiesta Amberstone in 1967. Both have a silk screen design on the lid and are unmarked. These are somewhat easy to find, but when purchasing, look over the dry part of the lid as well as the base. Glazes of butter dishes tend to discolor as a reaction from the butter.

VALUES: Casualstone and Amberstone Butter dish - length (base) 7 1/2" & (lid) 6 1/4"
        Antique Gold - $40   Brown - $20

There is no butter dish with Fiesta Ironstone.

The stick butter dish shown in new turquoise is from new Fiesta. It was introduced around 1990 and comes in all of the new colors except sapphire. This style is more in sync with Fiesta than the Amberstone/Casualstone butters of the late 60s. New Fiesta butter bases are marked with a Type VI mold mark.

VALUES: Lilac butters - $55-65

This is the standard Fiesta egg cup. It stands just a little over 3" tall and has an opening diameter of 3 3/8".

They were produced from 1936 until the mid 50s and come in 10 of the standard old Fiesta colors (no medium green since that color was not yet introduced.) They are not easy to find in any color, but the 50s colors are the scarcest.

VALUES: red - $75-85   lt. green, turq., yellow - $35-45
            cobalt, ivory - $50-60   50s colors - $125+

The Fiesta syrup is only found in the old line. The lid was made by the Dripcut company which produced various syrups and batter jugs. There are several versions of plastic lids made by various companies that often turn up on Fiesta bases. The Dripcut lid is the ONLY true lid for the Fiesta syrup.

Bases can be found with the Type IV mold mark.

VALUES: any color - $350+

There is only one style of ashtray in the Fiesta line. It is shown in two colors: brown from Fiesta Amberstone and light green. The ashtray was produced continuously from 1936 until 1969 and can be found in all of the old Fiesta colors as well as brown from Amberstone, gold from Casualstone. The Fiesta ashtray has a diameter of 5 1/2" and has a wet foot. There is no ashtray with Ironstone or the new Fiesta line and given today's public views on smoking, it is unlikely it will ever be reissued in any form.

The undersides of the ashtrays can be found in two different versions. The bottom ashtray is the "seven-ringed" variant which must have been produced from 1936 until before 1940 since they can be found in the first six colors only. There are seven rings on the very bottom, hence the name, and these ashtrays are unmarked.

The style on top is the most common. It has only two rings with room for a backstamp. These are found in all 11 colors (as well as amber and gold though they lack backstamps).

It is somewhat unusual to encounter an ashtray in a dinnerware line. Homer Laughlin produced several patterns which had ashtrays: Fiesta, Virginia Rose Dresden, OvenServe, and Harlequin. The last line mentioned having three distinct styles. The only ashtray that might cause some confusion is the Harlequin regular ashtray.

On the left is the Fiesta ashtray in red, to the right is the Harlequin regular ashtray in maroon. The ring pattern on the Harlequin regular ashtray is along the top of the inner wall. Fiesta's rings are located along the rim and on the very bottom of the inside. For more on Harlequin ashtrays, see section titled, Harlequin.

VALUES: Fiesta Ashtray

medium green - $150+	red and cobalt - $50
50s colors (rose at bottom end) - $75-90	original colors (excluding red & cobalt) - $35-40
Amberstone - $60	Casualstone - $30

Seldom does a dinnerware line include such accessory items as vases; especially for lines from the 30s and 40s considering there were dozens of potteries around that time that specialized in those types of items. Companies such as Hull, Roseville and McCoy were more apt to produce vases.

There are three sizes of the flower vase that was produced in the old Fiesta line. In the picture they are the 12" in ivory, 10" in red and 8" in light green. All three were introduced in mid 1936; the 12" and 10" were discontinued in 1942 and the 8" sometime around 1945. They can be found in the six original colors only. These are not impossible to find, but because of great demand, the prices are forced upward making the flower vases key pieces in a Fiesta collection.

VALUES: any color
　　　　12" - $1000+　(Type I mold mark)
　　　　10" - $600-700　(Type I mold mark)
　　　　 8" - $500-600　(Type I and IV mold marks)

　　　The 10" flower vase was the only size of the flower vases made in New Fiesta and was named, the Medium Vase. This is one of the items that causes the most confusion. Old and new 10" vases have at least two things in common: both have dry feet, both have identical Type I mold markings. The new 10" vase differes in thickness as a result of the difference in clay that is used today as compared to the 30s and 40s. The best way to determine if a 10" vase is old or new is to measure the height. New ones stand at most 9¾" (there are some seconds which will stand slightly smaller).

　　　On the left is the old 10" vase in light green and to the right is the new version in lilac. Remember the old vases were made only in red, cobalt, yellow, turquoise, light green and ivory, and stand almost exactly 10" tall.

　　　What if you are still not sure? Then, and this cannot be stressed enough, become familiar with the colors of Fiesta. Know the difference between the old and new versions of cobalt, turquoise, yellow. Know how to tell persimmon from red, seamist from light green, and ivory from new yellow.

　　　The Medium Vase of new Fiesta comes in all of the new Fiesta glazes. Lilac and sapphire are at the top of the price range. Lilac ones have gone for as much as $300 in mint condition with the original box. Sapphire, again, mint in box (MIB) average around $125. When Chartreuse is discontinued at the end of 1999, their prices should start to rise. Keep in mind that even though Apricot is now a discontinued color, it was in production for 11 years so apricot vases are not at all uncommon.

　　　The medium vase in chartreuse is a standard piece in the new Fiesta line the white 8" vase is an experimental. In 1986, the 8" vase was considered for production. Several trials were made in cobalt, black, white and possibly other colors. These were made using a lighter semi-vitreous clay, so if HLC decides to make 8" vases in the future in the heavy vitreous clay, then it should be easy in telling the difference between 1986 - 8" vase prototypes and any future examples.

VALUES: 8" vase in new colors (light semi-vitreous clay) - $1000+

Here are the old and new bud vases. On the left is the old version (6¼" tall) in red. To the right is the smaller (6" tall) new type in cobalt.

The bud vase was part of the 1936 original line and continued production until around 1945. Like the old flower vases, the bud vase can be found in the original six colors: red, cobalt, yellow, turquoise, light green, and ivory. These are much easier to find than the flower vases and have been found with Type I and Type IV mold markings.

VALUES: old Bud Vases
                red, cobalt - $95-115
                ivory, light green - $85-95
                turquoise, yellow - $50-75

New bud vases are taken directly from the old molds so they can be found with Type I and Type IV markings as well. New bud vases stand 6" tall and full ¼" smaller than the older versions. You will find new bud vases in every new color except sapphire – though several were made in sapphire and one is on display at HLC. White bud vases with red trim belong to a Christmas Fiesta line.

VALUES: Lilac Bud vases - $85+

On July 7, 1998, the Millennium I vase was modeled by Geisse. Sold exclusively through Bloomingdales, they were made in limited quantity: only 1000 in each of the following 10 colors: pearl gray, chartreuse, persimmon, cobalt, turquoise, periwinkle, rose, white, yellow, and sea mist, for a total of 10,000 vases.

The style of the Millennium I vase is more like a Grecian urn rather than the Art Deco/Streamline overall look of Fiesta. When these first hit eBay, collectors were shelling out upwards of $75+ to own an example. Now that a "cooling" off period has occurred, the Millennium I vase, or Milly I as it is affectionately called, average about $40 to $60. Keep in mind, these were limited to quantity. Though chartreuse may be more in demand, it should not be priced higher than the others just because the color is to be discontinued at the end of 1999.

Millennium II Vase A.K.A. Milly II was modeled on November 6, 1998, again by Geisse. There does not seem to be any middle ground with this vase: collectors either LOVE it or HATE it. Based on the disk pitcher, the Milly II was made as a limited edition item. Unlike the Milly I, Milly II will be made until the end of 1999.

Notice the new gray color on this piece. It tends to have a dark cast along the indented rings. Old gray is rather uniform and lacks this darkening effect around indentations.

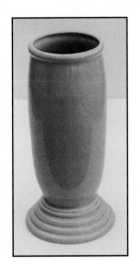

Left: Shown here in chartreuse, the Milly III vase, another example of Geisse's work, was modeled on November 12, 1998. It is based on an old experimental vase but it had to be redesigned because the opening would deform during production. The Milly III vase has a smaller opening resulting in a body that is more convex or curved. Like Milly's I and II, number III will be limited.

Right: This red vase is an experimental from the old line of Fiesta. It stands 12" tall and can be found in the main offices of Homer Laughlin under lock and key in a glass curio. It is also the basis for the Millennium III vase.

These utensils come from Fiesta Kitchen Kraft. They each have embossing on the handles and come from Oven Serve, a Homer Laughlin kitchenware line. The spoon and lifter (or cake knife as it is referred to in the modeling log) were modeled rather early August 1934 as part of the Oven Serve line. The salad fork came several years later in June of 1937.

Chips form easily on the ends due to use making all three items hard to find in mint condition. From left to right: cake server in cobalt, fork in yellow, spoon in light green. The fork and spoon were offered along with the unlisted salad bowl as part of a promotional offer. The three piece set, all in yellow, was available in the early 1940s for $1. Expect to find the utensils in the four colors of Fiesta Kitchen Kraft: yellow, light green, cobalt, and red.

VALUES: (any color) with measurements

Fork	length - 10"	widest part - 2³/4"	$100-115
Spoon	length - 9³/4"	widest part - 2³/4"	$100-115
Cake lifter	length - 9³/4"	widest part - 2¹/2"	$125-135

These three covered jars belong to the Fiesta Kitchen Kraft line. They were all listed as cookie jars in the modeling log. The first two versions of the large covered jar had handles; however, the handlelss version is the one which went into production.

These jars come in the Fiesta Kitchen Kraft colors: red, cobalt, yellow and light green. All three sizes should be marked with a Fiesta KK mold mark.

VALUES: (any color) with circumferences
Large, 27¹/2" - $275+
Medium, 22" - $200-225
Small, 14¹/2" - $275+

The refrigerator stack set is from the Fiesta Kitchen Kraft line. Like all KK items, the units and the lid lack the distinctive ring pattern found in the regular Fiesta line. These can be found in various combinations of red, cobalt, light green, and yellow. On very rare occasions, you may find them in ivory. Be aware, though, many white examples exist and both sellers and buyers confuse them for ivory. Kitchen Kraft items can be found in white (and sometimes ivory) with a multitude of different decal treatments. More than likely, the white examples are actually untreated blanks.

Lids are unmarked but sometimes can be found with an applied Fiesta Kitchen Kraft sticker. The units are marked with the Fiesta KK mold marking.

VALUES: (any color)
stacking lid - $55-65
unit (bowl) - $45-55

This is an experimental from New Fiesta: a refrigerator stack set consisting of two bowls in yellow and persimmon, and a lid in turquoise. Unlike the stack sets from old Fiesta Kitchen Kraft, this set was made with the bowls

having three small feet and a knobbed lid.

The lid was designed so that it could be interchangeable with the jumbo mug. I asked Mr. Parry why this very useful and well designed item was not put into production. He explains that retail clients who handle Fiesta are more apt to have interest in "showy" items such as Millennium vases rather than something utilitarian like the stack set.

Display signs were modeled in July of 1996. China Specialties, a company which decorates Fiesta products with "Moon Over Miami", "Mexicana," "Sunporch" and other treatments offers these display signs in various colors each year. So far they have been produced in persimmon, new turquoise, apricot, rose and chartreuse. Periwinkle display signs were also made, but these were actually intended to be turquoise.

The display sign is also used with various China Specialties treatments.

VALUES: Periwinkle (mistake glaze) - $40-45

Here is the original design of the new Fiesta Christmas ornament. The main difference is with the hanger which has a more open field. Breakage would occur during firing at the points where the hoop meets the body of the ornament. To overcome this, the open area was filled in resulting in a stronger hanger.

This is the modified version and the style that everyone should recognize. These were released for Christmas '97 in persimmon with gold Fiesta dancing lady, white with holly and white with cobalt Christmas tree. They were released again in 1998 and at the time of this writing may be issued again in chartreuse for Christmas of 1999.

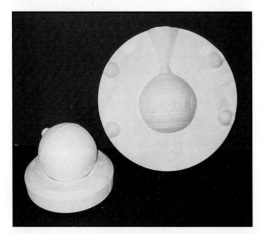

On the left is a dummy model and to the right is 1/2 of the actual mold of a ball shaped Christmas ornament that was being considered for New Fiesta. None were put into production.

Here we see several new Fiesta trials that could be confused as bowls turned upside down. They are pedestals which could be used for various purposes; from displaying other pieces of Fiesta to being used as bases for large candles.

Here are two of the small pedestals; bottom view in turquoise and top view in chartreuse. There were no pedestals made for old Fiesta.

Though you will not find these outside the plant, if you're curious, the dimensions are: Large Pedestal - base dia 7 3/4", top dia. 4 3/4", height 1 3/4"
Small Pedestal - base dia. 6 1/4", top dia. 4 1/2", height 1 5/8"

The trivet shown in a wooden disc pitcher shape board was modeled by Geisse. It is the only time the dancing lady was modeled on a piece of Fiesta. There are several companies that make what are called Genuine Fiesta Accessories. These include metal, plastic, and wood products fashioned with the Fiesta "look" to complement the dinnerware.

When an outside company wants to make a Fiesta accessory, they have to present the idea to HLC. This gives the pottery the opportunity to make the item itself should it choose. HLC toyed with the idea on making the trivets for the above item, however, it was later decided that imports from overseas could be used instead.

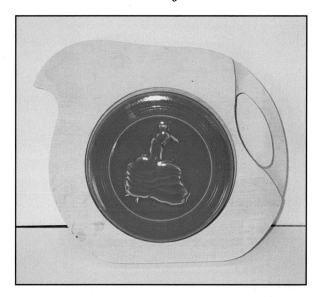

Fiesta with Treatments

Once in a while you may come across a piece of old Fiesta with some type of applied treatment. Fiesta with under the glaze red or blue stripes on an ivory body are very popular and usually command at least twice the normal price for an ordinary piece of ivory Fiesta.

Calendar plates are not too hard to find. They can be found in the 9" and 10" sizes for the years 1955 and 1954 in yellow, light green and ivory. The ivory 10" 1954 calendar plate is the easiest to find.

In 1962, white Fiesta with Hawaiian daisies was sold along with Fiesta pieces glazed in turquoise. A corresponding set was made in yellow with a stylized floral treatment. These sets were sold through the Plaid Stamp Company. The only items to receive the decoration were the 10", 7" plates, platter and saucer. These pieces are marked with an old Fiesta type inkstamp along with the word "CASUALS."

Turkey plates on 9", 10" and 13" plates are available. Shown with a yellow border is a 9" turkey plate.

VALUES: Turkey Plates
    9" - $55-65   13" - $100+
    10" - $75-85

New Fiesta with treatments are readily available. One popular treatment is called Quatro. It is a series of four colored bands featured on white Fiesta. The treatments found on new Fiesta are done by graphic designers, Judi Noble and Gordon Keiger.

This is called a Fiesta signature or dealer plate. They almost always appear on white, but some apricot and yellow examples were made.

"Looney Tunes" Fiesta made for Warner Bros. include Porky Pig on rose, Daffy Duck on new turquoise, Bugs Bunny on periwinkle, Tweety Bird on white, Scooby Doo on sea mist as well as several other characters. Shown is Sylvester on a yellow dinner plate.

There are two versions of Christmas Fiesta. The first has the holly treatment by itself. The second and more common has the holly with a red ribbon. These decals are done on white with a band of red trim. Some pieces meant to go with this line don't have the decal treatments, but will have the red trim such as shakers and the bud vase.

Special Christmas 9" plate made in 1998 for Federated Department Stores.

7" white Fiesta plate with the cobalt Christmas tree treatment. This decal can also be found on the Christmas ornaments.

This persimmon mug has received a decal treatment depicting a Christmas setting of Fiesta. These can be found in yellow, persimmon, periwinkle, white, turquoise, and sea mist green.

Two more of the various decaled new mugs.

Harlequin was made by Homer Laughlin as an F.W. Woolworth exclusive. Pieces for the line were first modeled in June of 1936 and in many cases, the early modeled pieces were referred to as Woolworth. The name Harlequin does not appear in the modeling log until February 1937. The line would be produced until 1964.

Though Harlequin was made by the same company and same designer and modelers, and even comes in many of the same colors as Fiesta, the overall shape and ring pattern is distinct. Harlequin rings are towards the center of pieces rather than along the rims like Fiesta's. Harlequin has a severe shape with conical bodies and tight, angular handles.

Only once in a while is Harlequin confused with Fiesta, and usually its the pieces of Harlequin that are more curved and less angled. This occurs more often with the ball jug, novelty creamer and individual salad bowl.

The "original eight" colors for Harlequin include: maroon, spruce green, a medium blue that many collectors have gotten into the habit of calling "mauve blue" (every non-HLC dinnerware line that has this shade calls this blue glaze, "medium blue" so I will use both terms to refer to the same color.) Harlequin yellow (brighter than Fiesta yellow), red, light green, turquoise and rose. Dark green, chartreuse, gray were available in the 50s along with rose, turquoise and yellow. (When referring to the "50s" colors, these include: dark green, gray and chartreuse ONLY.) Finally, medium green became a Harlequin color the same time it made its appearance in Fiesta in 1959.

The Fiesta colors ivory and cobalt were never standard colors in Harlequin, but once in a while a piece is found in those glazes. By the same token, maroon, mauve and spruce were never standard in Fiesta, but a few maroon Fiesta pieces have been found and there may be some in mauve and spruce.

After several versions of plates were designed for Harlequin, the hollow pieces were modeled. Interestingly, while they had the same ring pattern found in Harlequin, the first few prototypes were much more rounded.

The first few items modeled which have the familiar angular Harlequin look were the casserole, double egg cup and shaker.

Harlequin was reissued in 1979, again as a Woolworth exclusive. This time only four colors were used: turquoise, yellow, choral and green (collectors have fallen into the habit of calling this green "reissue green" to differentiate it from other greens, especially the old medium green glaze.) Yellow and turquoise are very close to their older versions while choral (bright red almost like new Fiesta's persimmon) was never offered in the old line.

Only nine items were used with this reissue Harlequin line and there is seldom trouble in telling old from new. For the most part, plates (and sometimes saucers) from the reissue line have an HLC backstamp. Old Harlequin was never marked.

Plates come in 10", 9", 7" and 6" sizes. Shown in yellow is the 10" version. All four sizes have the same ring pattern which the modeling log refers to as "in-the-ball." The ball part of the flat pieces is the area where the plate curves from the flat well to the rim.

The four sizes of plates come in all 12 standard colors. The 10" and 7" can also be found in the reissue colors and should be marked. Remember, old Harlequin pieces lack any type of marking.

VALUES: 10" plates

    original 8 colors - $24-26   medium green - $40-45

    50s colors - $30-35   reissue colors - $7-9

9" plates

    original 8 colors - $12-15   medium green - $40-45

    50s colors - $18-20

7" plates

    original 8 colors - $8-10   medium green - $18-20

    50s colors - $12-15   reissue colors - $3-6

6" plates

    original 8 colors - $6-8   medium green - $15-18

    50s colors - $10-12

Harlequin platters: 13" in red and 11" in yellow. Both sizes come in all twelve colors and were not part of the reissue line.

VALUES: either size

    original 8 colors - $20-25

    50s colors - $28-32

    medium green - $180+

Here are a few pieces of the reissue Harlequin in choral and reissue green. The large round platter was standard in choral, but it can also be found in yellow. Round platters were never made in the old Harlequin line.

VALUES: round chop plate/platter

    coral - $10-15

    yellow - $20-25

To the left is the oval baker in maroon. On the right is the round nappy in spruce green. Round nappies were made in reissue Harlequin. Reissue nappies were all supposed to have been made in reissue green, but many examples exist in yellow.

VALUES: Oval baker
    original 8 colors - $25-30

  Nappy
    original 8 colors - $18-20 reissue green - $8-10
    50s colors - $30-35   reissue yellow - $10-12
    medium green - $100+

Shown along side the Fiesta Individual salad bowl in medium green is the Harlequin salad bowl in turquoise. The most obvious difference is the wet foot on Harlequin as opposed to the dry foot on Fiesta.

Fiesta's individual salad bowl diameter - 7 3/4"   Harlequin's Ind. salad bowl diameter - 7 3/8"

VALUES: Harlequin Ind. salad bowl
    original 8 colors - $20-25 medium green - $85+
    50s colors - $32-36

The 36s bowl, shown in maroon, comes in all 12 Harlequin colors. Modeled in November of 1940, the 36s bowl was the last standard piece added to the Harlequin line (large cup would come later.) It is uncertain when maroon and spruce green were discontinued from Harlequin, but some believe it was not too long after the introduction of the 36s bowl since they are hard to find.

VALUES: 36s bowls
    original 8 colors - $20-25
    maroon, spruce - $65-75
    50s colors - $40-45
    medium green - $125+

The oatmeal and fruit bowls are similar in design and differ only in size. The oatmeal was part of reissue Harlequin and renamed "cereal soup bowl."

VALUES: 5 1/2" fruit bowl
        orig. 8 colors - $10-12
        50s colors - $15-18
        medium green - $40-45
     6 1/2" oatmeal
        orig. 8 colors - $18-20
        50s colors - $25-30
        medium green - $50-55
        reissue colors - $6-8

The nut dish was made in the first 8 colors only and is somewhat easy to find. This basket weave pattern used in Harlequin is actually a copy of a Japanese import.

On the right is a Harlequin nut dish in light green (not the easiest color to find in Harlequin nut dishes). To the left is the Japanese version in green with a dark band and red flowers.

A stack of nut dishes in all the available colors.

VALUES:
    colors other than light green - $25-30
    light green - $40+

The Harlequin cream soup cup can be found in all 12 colors. Harlequin cream soups in the 50s colors (chartreuse, gray and dark green) and medium green are rarest. Most of the Harlequin and Fiesta items were modeled by Kraft, but the cream soup was done by Berrisford on February 1938. It is listed as item 1045 with dimensions as 5¹/₈" x 2" and is listed as having a capacity of 11.15 oz. There is a note written to the side that this item was released on March 15, 1938.

VALUES: original 8 colors - $30   medium green - $850+
50s colors - $50+

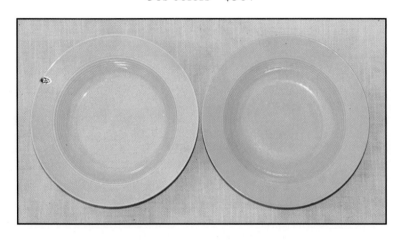

The 8" deep plate comes in all 12 colors. Here it is shown in *both* Harlequin and Fiesta yellows. It is not too uncommon to find both Harlequin and Riviera in Fiesta yellow which is a darker glaze. The Harlequin yellow deep plate on the left has its original 20 cent sticker.

VALUES: 8" deep plate
original 8 colors - $20-25
50s colors - $40-45
medium green - $90-100

Here is a comparison of two Harlequin teacups in coral and rose. The Coral example on the left comes from reissue Harlequin. The rose teacup on the right is from the old Harlequin line.

The After Dinner cup (#1320) was modeled in September of 1939 by Kraft. These can be found in all of Harlequin colors (shown here in rose) with medium green being especially scarce.

VALUES: A.D. cups
original 8 colors - $50   med green - $325+
50s colors - $100+
A.D. Saucers
original 8 colors - $10   med. green - $60+
50s colors - $25+

The various cups and saucers available in Harlequin: far left: AD up in yellow, AD saucer in turquoise; center: chartreuse large cup; far right: teacup in red, regular saucer in dark green.

Teacups and saucers come in all 12 old colors and the four reissue glazes. They are among the easiest pieces of Harlequin to find. On the other hand, the large cup is rather scarce. The body lacks any type of ring pattern.

VALUES:

teacups:	original 8 colors - $8-10	medium green - $20-25
	50s colors - $12-15	reissue colors - $4-6
saucers:	original 8 colors - $3-5	medium green - $10-12
	50s colors - $6-8	reissue colors - $1-2
large cups:	any color - $200+	

From left to right: Harlequin tumblers in mauve, rose and maroon. Referred to as "mug" in the model log, the Harlequin tumbler can be found in the first eight colors of Harlequin: red, light green, mauve blue, yellow, rose, spruce green, maroon, and turquoise. Modeled by Kraft in December of 1937, the tumbler is listed as item 1019 and having a capacity of 11½ oz.

VALUES: any color - $35-40

The regular creamer comes in all 12 colors as well as turquoise from the reissue line.

VALUES: original 8 colors - $10-12
50s colors - $15-18
medium green - $60-70

The high lip creamer must have been the first piece of Harlequin to be discontinued since it can be found in the first four colors of Harlequin only: maroon, mauve blue, spruce green and Harlequin yellow. There are two styles of lips for this item; the one shown in maroon and another which has the lip extending to half-way around the top of the creamer.

VALUES: either style, any color - $150+

Look for the band of rings on the side and a set of rings on the underside of this *Novelty Creamer*. This will let you know if you have a piece of Harlequin or not.

VALUES: original 8 colors - $20-25
50s colors - $30-35
medium green - $1200+

Shown in maroon is what HLC documents list as a toy creamer. It was made for Woolworth and can be found in the first eight Harlequin colors: maroon, yellow, mauve blue, spruce green, red, rose, turquoise and light green. These will have a completely dry underside (wiped foot).

VALUES: original 8 colors - $20-25

Here are the two different styles of sugars found in Harlequin. The one on the right in red is from the original line made from the beginning of production until it was discontinued in 1964. It can be found in all twelve colors.

There is a set of rings on the inside wall. You can also find variations of rings on the inside bottom. Some have a set of three narrowly spaced rings, other will have the rings widely spaced. There is also a variation which has the inside bottom rings widely spaced with a "dot" in the center. The last variant has NO rings on the inside bottom and these are toward the end of Harlequin's production.

The sugar on the left in yellow is from the reissue line of Harlequin, a.k.a. Harlequin Ironstone. The finial and handles are "filled in" rather than open. This was done to make production more efficient. The handles and lid finial are actually part of the mold, eliminating the need to produce them separately and then apply them by hand.

Dimensions for both sugars are the same: lid diameter - 4⁵/₈"; base height - 2⁵/₈"; opening diameter - 4¹/₄".

VALUES: Old style sugar:

original 8 colors - $20-25	medium green - $125+
50s colors - $35-40	Reissue sugar in yellow - $10-15

Shown in red and spruce green, the Harlequin salt and pepper shakers come in all 12 Harlequin colors. It is somewhat curious these were not part of the Woolworth anniversary in the late 70s. They stand 3¹/₂" tall. The salt shaker can be distinguished from the pepper by the size of the holes. The spruce green shaker has its original 15-cent sticker. These stickers can be found in various values gracing pieces of Harlequin and Riviera.

VALUES: (for PAIR)

original 8 colors - $15-20
50s colors - $30-32
medium green - $200+

Here the Harlequin shakers are found with an all-over floral gold design. This was not done at Homer Laughlin. More than likely this was done by Pearl China, a company which excelled at gold decoration. It really is hard to say though. There were many small potteries in the surrounding area and some, my grandfather included, had kilns in their basements. Gold decoration was a very easy way of covering up another potters mistake or production flaw. The original color of the spruce green can be seen inside both shakers.

Sauceboats are easy to find and come in all 12 Harlequin colors. It was modeled by Kraft in April of 1938 and records indicate its capacity at 15 1/2 oz.

VALUES: original 8 colors - $15-18
50s colors - $25-30
medium green - $175+

Marmalades come in the first eight colors. Modeled by Berrisford in Feb. 1937, its capacity is listed as 93/4 oz.

VALUES: any color - $255+

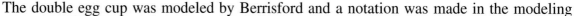

The double egg cup was modeled by Berrisford and a notation was made in the modeling book that it was released on July 28th 1936. It can be found in all 12 glazes. The smaller of the two cups has a dry ring. Measurements are: large cup opening diameter - 23/4"; small cup opening diameter - 33/4".

VALUES:
original 8 colors - $18-20
50s colors - $30-35
medium green - $200+

Single egg cup, or individual egg cup in yellow. These are not too hard to find in the first eight colors (except for light green).

VALUES: any color - $25-30

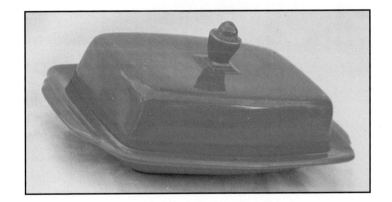

The 1/2 lb. butter dish is a borrowed piece from an already existing HLC line, Jade. These butterdishes were also sold with Riviera and since they are found in cobalt, many collectors believe they were sold with Fiesta as well. In Harlequin's case, they come in the first eight colors.

VALUES: any color - $125-150

The Harlequin casserole comes in the first 11 colors only – no medium green. This was one of the first pieces of Harlequin to be designed with the characteristic angular body and handles. It was modeled as, "STRAIGHT SIDED CASSEROLE" by Kraft in August of 1936.

VALUES:
    original 8 colors - $90-110
    50s colors - $150+
    medium green - $500+

Here in spruce green is Harlequin teapot. They come in all 12 colors. As with any teapot, look over the spout and the opening for the lid as that is where damage is likely to occur.

VALUES: original 8 colors - $150-175
50s colors - $200+
medium green - $500+

There have been dozens of potteries that have made ball jugs throughout the years. The ball jug shown here was sold with Harlequin even though it has the Fiesta style rings around the base. It was modeled on July of 1937 by Berrisford. Interestingly, it is listed in the modeling log, ". . . as Hall china."

Hall china ball jugs are in abundance and can be found in solid colors, with decals (very common in the popular Autumn Leaf pattern), and with gold decoration. The Hall China ball jugs do not have any ring configuration and most of the time are marked.

McCoy produced a ball jug in solid colors which *does* have a similar ring pattern. It is easy to tell the difference, though, since McCoy ball jugs will have a completely dry foot.

The Harlequin ball jug can be found in all 12 colors, though extremely rare in medium green.

VALUES: original 8 colors - $65-75
50s colors - $125+
medium green - $1800+

Here is the underside of the Harlequin ball jug. It will either have a dry foot ring, or a wet foot with three sagger pin marks as this one does. Notice the set of rings towards the base.

The 22 oz. Jug is listed in the model log as being modeled by Kraft on March 1938. It is listed as item 1066 with a capacity of 22.5 oz. and being released on May 10, 1938. These jugs are not too hard to find in excellent condition. Prices seem to reflect high demand rather than availability. They come in all 12 Harlequin colors with medium green being virtually non existent.

VALUES: all colors except turquoise and yellow - $60-75
             turquoise and yellow - $40-50
             medium green - $500+

The Harlequin relish tray is much harder to find than its Fiesta counterpart. The unmarked base is similar to Fiesta's but it has a set of Harlequin like rings and has been found in turquoise only.

VALUES: relish base (turquoise only) - $50-55
           relish section: any color - $42-47

There are three styles of Ashtrays in the Harlequin line: regular, basket weave and ashtray/saucer. The maroon ashtray is the regular version which is found in the first 8 colors.

VALUES: any color - $50+

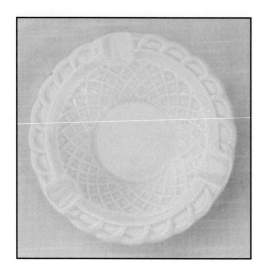

The basket weave, like the basket weave nut dish, was copied from a Japanese import. Shown in Harlequin yellow, it was modeled by Kraft in August of 1939 and released on December of that year. They come in all 12 Harlequin colors.

VALUES: original 8 colors - $35+
50s colors - $100+
medium green - $250+

Shown here in spruce green with a red teacup, the ashtray saucer was made at the same time as the Basketweave style. Of all the Harlequin ashtrays, this is the hardest to find. A rare few have turned up in ivory − not a standard Harlequin color.

VALUES: any color - $60-70
ivory - $150-200

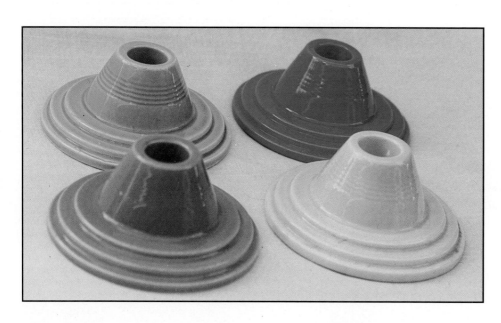

Shown is the only style of candlesticks available in Harlequin, though two other versions were modeled. They are rather scarce and can be found in the first seven colors of Harlequin: mauve blue, Harlequin yellow, maroon, spruce green, red, turquoise, and rose. In the picture: back: turquoise and red; front: mauve blue and Harlequin yellow.

VALUES: any color (PAIR) - $300+

In the late 70s and early 80s Homer Laughlin issued a line of dinnerware called Table Fair to be sold in grocery stores. It used several of the Harlequin shapes including: 10" plate, 7" plate, round serving bowl and the cereal soup bowl. The pieces were glazed in an ivory/white color and decorated with brown specks. The 10" and 7" plates received a brown stamp design along the rim as well as a treatment of either strawberries or wheat stalks.

Other items from Table Fair that don't use Harlequin shapes are: gravy, cup/mug, saucer, covered butter, casserole, covered sugar, creamer and coffeepot. Most Table Fair is marked Homer Laughlin.

These pieces are very easy to find in the west coast and can be purchased in many thrift shops in California for next to nothing.

Shown here is a cup and saucer, 10" plates with and without decoration, a butter dish and a round serving bowl.

Table Fair 10" plate, cereal soup bowl, gravy dish, and a 7" plate.

Harlequin Animals

Harlequin animals are highly desirable by not only Harlequin collectors, but Fiesta and HLC collectors as well. Six animals make up the set: penguin, duck, lamb, cat, donkey, and fish in the Harlequin colors of Harlequin yellow, spruce green, mauve blue and maroon.

VALUES: for any animal in standard glaze - $150-175

The fish (from left to right) in yellow, maroon, and spruce green.

The lamb in yellow.

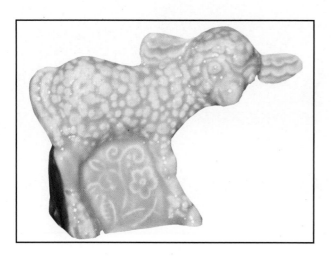

Lamb in Fiesta's turquoise glaze. This variant has its front leg closer to the flower than the standard production lamb.

The duck in spruce green.

A pair of penguins in yellow and maroon.

Here is a penguin in turquoise. This variant has a small head and little feet giving it a much more realistic look than the more familiar "big head/big feet" penguin.

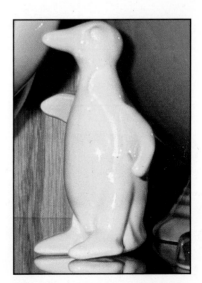

Side view of small head/feet penguin. These, along with the turquoise lamb, are on display at Homer Laughlin. None in solid colors have been found outside the plant.

The donkey in mauve blue.

The donkey in gold. Many of the Harlequin animals were decorated outside the factory by various companies. Some can be found with their original Harlequin color with gold trim; others are done completely in gold like the donkey seen here.

The cat in mauve blue.

Here are two cats which are called Mavericks. These are not produced at HLC, but rather by some other company. You will find Maverick versions of all six Harlequin animals: they are generally smaller and do not come in the same glazes as the real HLC Harlequin animals. The cat on the left is in a cobalt blue which is much lighter than the cobalt used in Fiesta and the cat on the right has cold paint (decorative paint over the glaze) that is chipping off. Mavericks are worth considerably less than Harlequin animals.

Here are original molds. On the left is half a mold for the duck, and on the right is half a mold for the donkey.

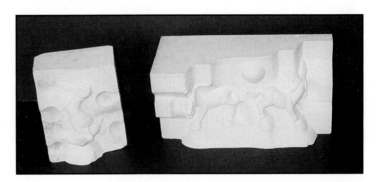

When Harlequin was being reissued in the late 1970s, a test run of the Harlequin animals was done. These were never mass produced and never sold to the public. The cat is in the yellow glaze used in reissue Harlequin. Recently, some animals have been found in reissue green. All other animals shown are in a clear glaze.

You will find various look-alikes that have been made through the years. McCoy made a lamb planter very similar to the Harlequin lamb, but it is much larger. However, in many cases, knock-offs are smaller than the originals.

Though its the right size, the donkey lacks the sharp details found on the Harlequin version. Here, this look-a-like, along with its cart, make up a salt and pepper set.

The peach colored cat also lacks details and has a hole in its back. The inside bottom is lined with a piece of styrofoam so this is more than likely a novelty vase.

Riviera, HLC's third most collected line of colorware, was first made in 1938. Many of the shapes used in Riviera come from the Century line which had already been in production.

The colors used in Riviera are: red, mauve/medium blue, Harlequin yellow, light green and ivory. Once in a while a piece is found in Fiesta yellow. Turquoise juice tumblers and 1/4 lb. butters are available. Cobalt platters, plates are not too hard to find and at least one of each of the following is known in the dark blue glaze: sugar, creamer, casserole.

Century is a square shaped line with saw-tooth like corners. Several companies produced similar ware during the 30s including W.S. George and Leigh Potters. HLC's extensive line of Century was used for decal treatments. Shown is a Mexicana decal from the late 30s.

Most of the pieces in Riviera come from Century, but not all. The ones that do include:

all size platters	all size plates	deep plate	teapot
teacup	saucer	sauceboat	syrup
batter jug	casserole	creamer	sugar
oatmeal bowl	nappies	fruit bowl	bakers

You may find many other Century pieces in ivory with decals or in plain ivory, but they do not belong to the Riviera line.

Pieces made especially for Riviera include:

handled tumbler	juice pitcher	juice tumbler	1/4 lb. butter

Records indicate a compartment plate was made in 1940 and revised several times, but they must not have been put into mass production.

Finally, a few items were borrowed from other lines such as the Jade 1/2 lb. butter and the Tango shakers.

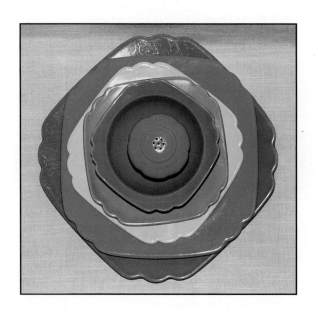

Shown here are various sizes of plates with a saucer and shaker on top.

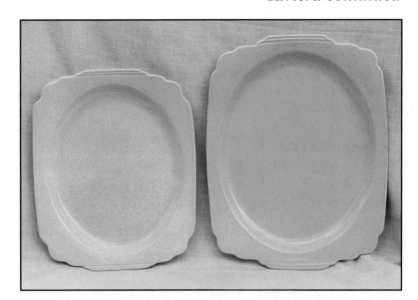

Handled platters with oval wells.

Shown here is a cobalt handled platter with mauve/medium blue unhandled platter – again with oval wells. You will also find some platters with square or rectangular wells.

To the left in light green is the oval baker. This particular example is known as the curved side baker. The other style, not shown, is the straight side baker. Both are 9" in length and the curved side baker has a more rounded well whereas the straight side version has a more rectangular well.

On the right in yellow is the 7 1/4" nappy. These are rather easy to find, especially in red. Unfortunately, like all Riviera, the undersides chip easily because of its thin body.

At the left is an oatmeal bowl which measures 6" in diameter and on the right is a 5 1/2" fruit cup.

Shown here are two deep plates. The one on the left is Fiesta yellow, the one on the right is Harlequin yellow.

Here are the sugar and creamer for Riviera. There are no other styles for either item. Shown in red, they can be found also in light green, mauve blue, yellow and ivory. Creamers are much easier to find than sugars.

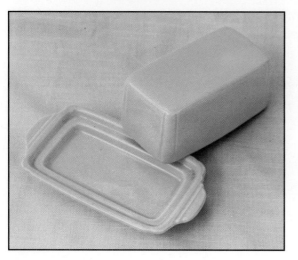

Unlike the 1/2 lb. butter, the 1/4 lb. size was designed specifically for Riviera. It is believed that these were sold with Fiesta (but not as Fiesta) since in addition to the Riviera colors of red, light green, yellow (as shown), mauve blue and ivory, they can be found in turquoise and cobalt. The base measures 6 1/4" by 3 1/4" and the lid's dimensions are: 4 1/2" by 2 1/4" by 2".

The 1/2 lb. butter from Jade which was used with Harlequin was also used with Riviera.

This large batter jug is hard to find with a lid. Ivory, red and light green lids are the only colors known for this piece.

The covered syrup, shown in red, is one of the harder pieces of Riviera to find. They are generally part of batter sets which consist of the syrup, a covered batter jug, and a platter.

Riviera juice set, left to right, tumblers in mauve blue, yellow, light green, mauve blue juice pitcher, tumblers in red, ivory and turquoise.

Both the pitcher and the tumblers from the Riviera juice set are hard to find. When found, the pitchers are generally yellow, but once in a while mauve blue or red ones pop up.

The tumblers are similar in size to

the Fiesta juice tumblers. Only the 1/4 lb. and 1/2 lb. butterdishes and the juice tumbler can be found in turquoise.

This grouping of handled mugs shows the four colors of Riviera: red, mauve blue, light green and Harlequin yellow. Unlike other items of Riviera which came from Century, the handled mug was designed specifically for Riviera. Modeled by Kraft in February of 1939. It is listed as model number 1194 and having a capacity of 10.5 oz.

Even though they were not made for Century, they can be found in ivory. Some Riviera collectors speculate that when red was discontinued in 1943, ivory took its place.

An overhead view of the Tango shape shakers used in Riviera. Tango's colors include red, yellow, mauve/medium blue, maroon and spruce green, so if you find shakers in those last two colors, they don't belong to Riviera.

An ivory Riviera teapot.

RIVIERA ITEMS AND VALUES:

Prices are for red, light green, ivory, yellow, mauve/medium blue. Cobalt items can go from 2X to 4X listed prices.

10" plate - $40-45

9" plate - $12-15

7" plate - $8-10

6" plate - $6-8

5 1/2" fruit cup - $12-15

6" oatmeal bowl - $20-25

nappy - $20-25

baker (either style) - $25-30

deep plate - $15-18

covd. sugar - $20+

creamer - $10-15

cup - $12-15

saucer - $4-6

covered syrup - $150+

gravyboat - $25-30

shakers, pr. - $15-18

handled tumbler - $60+   (Ivory - $120+)

juice tumbler - $50-60

juice pitcher - $95-115 (yellow)

$250+ colors other than yellow

batter jug, w/o lid - $75-85

batter jug, w/lid - $150-175

1/2 lb. covd. butter - $125-150

1/4 lb. covd. butter: red - $125

turq./cobalt - $257+

any other color - $90-110

teapot - $85-100

casserole - $95-125

platters, closed handles, any size - $25-30

platters, open handles, any size - $40-45

Carnival was produced by Homer Laughlin for the Quaker Oats Company. In fact Homer Laughlin produced several lines for Quaker Oats which included decalware lines of Harvest, Tea Rose, Wild Rose as well as others. Two lines came in colored glazes: Carnival and OvenServe.

Like the other promotional lines, Carnival is very limited. Five shapes make up the line: tea cup, saucer, 6" plate, fruit bowl and oatmeal bowl. The only decoration is a set of two indented rings along the rim.

According to the Carnival Oats boxes, there seems to be two groupings of Carnival: 30s and 50s. The 30s grouping, which probably continued into the early 40s makes use of the colors: red, cobalt, light green, ivory and Fiesta yellow. The 50s grouping is made up of the colors: turquoise, gray, dark green and Harlequin yellow.

Certain colors for certain items are easier to find than others. Cups seem to be rather common in turquoise, yellow, gray, dark green and ivory. Fruit and cereal bowls are easy to find in turquoise and yellow. Light green and yellow are the dominate colors for the 6" plates. Cobalt and red saucers are not too readily available, but more so than other items in those colors.

Carnival is very light weight compared to other HLC wares. As a result, damage such as chips and cracks occur often. There is a good side, however. It is very easy to find, both in antique shops and on online auctions. There are various opinions on whether one should buy damaged items or not. For rare or experimental items, some damage can be overlooked. When it comes to Carnival, unless you have to have it right when you see it, there is no problem in passing it over. With minimal patience, this line is very easy to collect in MINT condition.

There are no markings found on Carnival. The simple design and limited nature of this line prevents it from being confused with other colorware; the only exception would be Deanna produced by Knowles. Even here there should be no problem since Deanna flatware has three raised rings as opposed to Carnival's indented pair.

Here is a Mother's Carnival Oats box. It comes from the 1950s since the colors of gray and dark green were produced by Homer Laughlin during that time period. There are also other Quaker Oats boxes, one of which shows Carnival in colors from the 1940s and another has small Oven Serve items illustrated.

Fruit Bowls in turquiose and red; 51/2"
Fruit bowls - $5

Oatmeal Bowls in yellow,
gray and turquoise; 61/8"
Oatmeal bowls, 61/8" diameter - $4

Plates in dark green, light green, cobalt,
yellow, gray and turquoise; 65/8"
65/8" plates - $4

Tea cups gray with yellow saucer:
   cups - $5
   saucers - $2

Collectors of HLC's Carnival are always on the look out for larger items such as plates and platters. I could find no evidence that any were modeled but some are adamant that these pieces are out there.

To the right is the standard Carnival teacup in turquoise. On the left is a cup in red that was made by Homer Laughlin and is very similar to Carnival. This red cup is listed in the modeling log as a "Sellers" cup and was modeled in February of 1939 for M. Sellers, a west coast distributor for HLC.

The most obvious difference is in the handles: the Sellers handle is more curved than Carnival's. The two cups have similar, but not identical bodies. The red Sellers cup has five raised rings in comparison to Carnival's three.

Sellers cups can be found in various colors, but they are not nearly as common as its Carnival counterpart. Saucers are available for Sellers cups: they have a set of equally spaced rings towards the center of the cup well.

VALUES: Sellers cup (any color) - $65
Sellers saucer (any color) - $25

Oven Serve

Oven Serve is a rather ornate embossed line that was produced by BOTH Homer Laughlin and Taylor, Smith and Taylor. TS & T produced smaller items such as custard cups, small bakers, and handled bowls or ramekins. HLC's version of Oven Serve was much more extensive with pie plates, casseroles, pitchers and bowls. Many of these exotic items are found with decal treatments or hand-painted work on the raised part. All of HLC's Oven Serve can be found in pumpkin (orange) and yellow.

The smaller items produced by both HLC and TS & T are very easy to find in solid colored glazes of pink, brown, turquoise, dark green, yellow, pumpkin (a dull orange glaze) and white.

Here is the HLC Oven Serve cup and saucer in yellow. This particular example was sold on eBay for a little over $100. Pumpkin cups and saucers are worth considerably less.

The handled bowl a.k.a. ramekin in pumpkin, the 9 1/2" plate in yellow nd a turquoise 5 1/2" bowl all produced by HLC. HLC's handled bowl differs from TS & T's by the handle. TS & T's will begin at the rim of the bowl rather than down on the side like HLC's.

VALUES: 9 1/2" plate: (HLC)
yellow - $20-25
pumpkin - $12-15
5 1/2" bowl (HLC or TS&T) - $5-7
Handled bowl (HLC or TS&T), any color - $6-8

The oval baker was another small item produced by both TS & T and HLC. Both companies marks can be found in the form of an inkstamp as well as an in-the-mold-mark.

VALUES: Small oval baker: (HLC or TS & T) - $8-10

There are two sizes of shirred egg dishes. Shown in the pumpkin glaze is the smaller of the two measuring 7" from tab to tab. The term "Shirred" means ". . . to cook (unshelled eggs) until set."

VALUES: shirred egg dish (HLC) - $20-25

Custards and Ramekins

VALUES: (HLC or TS & T) - $5-7

Plates - 9", 7", and 6"

VALUES: 9" Plate   yellow - $20-25
                          pumpkin - $12-15
              7" Plate   yellow - $14-18
                          pumpkin - $8-10
              6" Plate   yellow - $10-12
                          pumpkin - $5-8

This oven Serve jug is on display at HLC.

Lu-Ray Pastels was made by the Taylor Smith & Taylor China company (commonly initialed TS & T or TST) rom 1938 until 1961. Both the style and color assortment was a departure from other solid colored dinnerware lines of the late 30s. Lu-Ray's pastel shades were lighter and softer than the bold Fiesta-like colors and the shapes used in Lu-Ray lacked geometrical Art Deco design.

It was common practice for TS & T to redesign the hollowware of an existing line and "recycle" the flat pieces. Such was the case with two lines which would be used with Lu-Ray: Laurel and Empire. Laurel was offered from 1933 until the mid 50s. Some flat pieces such as platters had decorative tab handles as did bakers and tab handled soup bowls.

In 1936, Empire hollowware was made such as teapots, creamers, sugars, casseroles, etc. The flatware for Empire was taken from Laurel. So while the hollow pieces to Empire and Laurel are distinct, the flat pieces such as plates, saucers, and platters are shared.

Technically, Lu-Ray is the Empire shape in pastel glazes, but many collectors still cite the flat pieces as coming from Laurel. Then there are many pieces designed especially for Lu-Ray like the teacup, egg cup and mixing bowls.

The original colors for Lu-Ray are: Persian Cream (yellow), Windsor Blue, Surf Green, and Sharon Pink. In the rest of this section "4 original colors" will refer to these glazes and instead of using the official names over and over, they will simply be called, yellow, blue, green and pink.

Chatham gray was offered in 1948 and didn't last into 1953. By this time, many Lu-Ray pieces had been discontinued and are not found in gray today. In general, gray Lu-Ray is rare and is priced very high (gray is to Lu-Ray as medium green is to Fiesta.)

The Lu-Ray backstamp which appears on virtually very Lu-Ray piece. There is no in-the-mold mark for any Lu-Ray item.

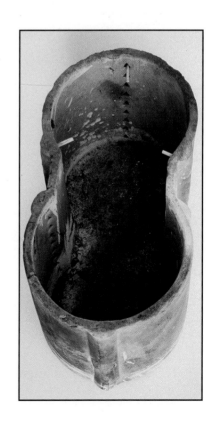

Old sagger with pins on top row.

This is an old sagger which came from the TS & T factory. Each circular section has three rungs of holes for pins. Notice the three pins on the top of one of the circular sections. This is how sagger pin marks form on the underside of flatware. "Shelves" of plates could be put in one of these saggers and could be fired at the same time.

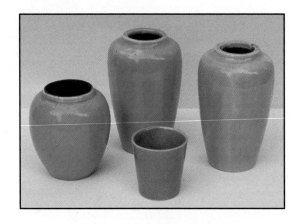

These small vases are test glaze pieces. It was recently confirmed that TS & T used the pink and gray examples shown.

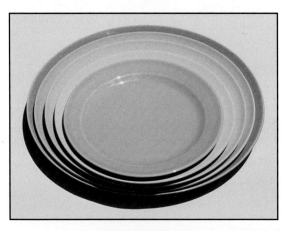

You will find five sizes of plates in the Lu-Ray line. They measure (from smallest to largest): 6 1/4", 71/2", 81/2", 91/2" and 101/2".

VALUES:	4 original colors	gray
10"	$18-22	$25-30
9"	$10-12	$18-22
8"	$18-22	$40-45
7"	$8-10	$18-22
6"	$6-8	$12-15

All five sizes come in all five colors. The 9" and 6" sizes are the most common. The 8", especially in gray, is the hardest to find. 8" plates were used as an underplates for the muffin covers.

Having a diameter of 14", the chop plate comes in all five colors and is very rare in gray.

VALUES:	4 original colors	gray
	$30-35	$600-800

Look for the familiar Laurel tab handles on this cake plate. They have a diameter of 103/4" and were never made in gray.

VALUES: 4 original colors - $65-85

Shown are compartment plates (Grill plates) in gray and pink. These come in all five colors and may or may not be marked. They have a diameter of 10". On the back you may notice a double foot. This is to give the plate added strength for the extra weight produced by the divisions on the surface.

VALUES: 4 original colors - $30-35
                      gray - $100-125

11" blue platter on a 13" yellow platter. Both sizes come in all five Lu-Ray colors and both have decorative tab handles.

VALUES: either size
                      4 original colors - $15-20
                      gray - $40-50

Both of these shapes are Laurel flatware which was also used in Empire. They, like the larger platters, have decorative tab handles.

In green is the pickle. It measures 9½" across and comes in the first four colors only (no gray). The pickle is sometimes called a relish, celery or sauceboat liner.

The small 7" platter, shown in pink, is very hard to find.

VALUES: Pickle: 4 original colors - $30-35
                      7" platter: any color - $400-500

Here are two styles of teacups found in Lu-Ray. The first version is on the left. It has a blunt stubby foot, "straight" sides and its handle is placed low on the body. The second version, in pink, has a distinctive foot, flared sides and high handle placement.

The first version is much harder to find and it is believed the second style replaced the first very early in production.

Unlike many other pieces of Lu-Ray the cups did not come from a preexisting line; they were designed *for* Lu-Ray. Most collectors find it surprising the teacup does not exactly fit the indentation of the saucer. The Lu-Ray teacup saucer is the same one used in both Empire and Laurel. Why a new saucer wasn't made for the new style cup is unknown.

From left to right: teacup and saucer in yellow, A.D. cup and saucer in gray, chocolate cup and saucer in pink. This picture shows the three types of cups and saucers found in Lu-Ray. The chocolate cup on the far right was part of the chocolate set. It, along with every other chocolate set item, was replaced very early in Lu-Ray's production and is very hard to find today. Because it was available for such a brief time, they do not come in gray.

The A.D. cup and saucer in the middle, like the teacup, was designed especially for Lu-Ray, but they can be found in later lines including Dwarf Pine (a pastel pink line with pine cone spray decal) and in white with various treatments. They can be found in all five Lu-Ray colors and are much easier to find than the chocolate cups and saucer.

VALUES:	original 4 colors	gray
regular teacup	$10-15	$30-35
regular saucer	$5-6	$10-12
A.D. cup	$20-25	$40-45
A.D. saucer	$12-15	$18-22
chocolate cup	$100+	—
chocolate saucer	$50-60	—

All three bowls shown here are from both Laurel and Empire. Having the same general style, they differ only in size.

In the background is the coupe soup or deep plate in gray. It has a diameter of 7³/₄" and comes in all five colors.

To the left in the foreground is one of the most common pieces of Lu-Ray, the fruit cup. It has a diameter of 5¹/₄".

To the right of the very common fruit cup is a VERY RARE 6¹/₂" bowl in green. Very few of these have been accounted for. One collector has several – all in green.

VALUES:	4 original colors	gray
Coupe soup	$15-20	$35-40
5¹/₄" fruit cup	$6-8	$30-35
6¹/₂" bowl	$300-400	—

36s Bowls. The term "36s" refers to a specific size of bowl. In the old days of pottery making, there were various sizes including 12s, 24s, etc. The numbers specify how many bowls of that particular size could fit into a barrel. The larger the bowl, the smaller the number.

36s bowls were common pieces in many dinnerware lines up until the 1950s. In the Lu-Ray line, they can be found in all five colors (as shown) with gray being the most difficult to find.

VALUES: 4 original colors - $40-55   gray - $100-150

In yellow is the cream soup cup with liner and to the right is a lug soup in gray. Both were original to the line, but the cream soup with liner was discontinued first before 1948 when gray became a Lu-Ray color. The cream soup, which is much harder to find than the lug soup, along with its 6½" liner comes in the first four colors only.

The more common lug soup comes in all five colors. Look for the Laurel decorative tab handles on the lug soup.

VALUES: cream soup cup: 4 original colors - $45-60
cream soup saucer: 4 original colors - $25-30
lug soup: 4 original colors - $18-25
lug soup: gray - $50-55

Oval bakers come in all five Lu-Ray colors. Some collectors make a distinction between two types. On the left in green is the version with a tapered foot. The pink baker on the right has a flat underside. Both styles seem to have been made simultaneously. The baker is a Laurel shape and will have the raised decorative tab handles on either side. Actual measurements are: 10¾" by 7¾".

VALUES: (either style)
4 original colors - $18-20
gray - $40-45

Here are nappies in all five Lu-Ray colors. They have a diameter of 8³/₄" and are not too hard to find.

VALUES: 4 original colors - $18-20
                gray - $40-45

Shown here in all five Lu-Ray colors are the salad bowls. First offered in 1941, the salad bowls measure 10" in diameter and are extremely rare in gray. In Lu-Ray circles, only three or four gray salads are known to exist.

VALUES: 4 orig. colors - $50-65
             gray - $600-800

The mixing bowls were introduced in 1941. Mr. Smith explained these bowls could not be made cheap enough to compete with other companies which specialized in making kitchenware. As a result, they were made for a very brief period of time. These bowls were made specifically for Lu-Ray and though discontinued sometime in the 1940s they would later make a return in the Pebbleford glazes.

The four sizes are: 10¹/₂", 8¹/₂", 7" and 5¹/₂".

Collectors have noticed that certain sizes in certain colors are hard to find. The two larger bowls are easier to find in blue and yellow whereas the two smaller bowls are easier to find in green and pink.

VALUES:

10¹/₂" or 8¹/₂":
blue or yellow - $200-250 ea.
pink or green - $300 ea.

7" or 5¹/₂":
blue or yellow - $300 ea.
pink or green - $200-250 ea.

Here are the original demitasse pieces offered in Lu-Ray. The "straight sided" coffeepot, creamer, sugar, cup and saucer were all generic shapes already in production which did not belong to any particular line. All of these shapes would be discontinued after the first year of production and replaced by "curved" shapes more in tune with the Empire shape.

Here are the shapes that replaced the "straight sided" set. The coffeepot, A.D. sugar and A.D. creamer have all the design elements of Empire. The A.D. cup, like the teacup, was designed for Lu-Ray. Unlike the teacup saucer which was taken from Empire/Laurel, the A.D. saucer was made specially for the A.D. cup.

When these sets were made, they were commonly called, "after dinner" or "demitasse" sets. The pieces would have been called "individual" as in individual creamer or individual sugar to differentiate from their regular counterparts.

The term "chocolate pot" refers to a small and very ornate coffee pot from the turn of the century. They are usually found with flowing lines, elaborate gold trim and hand painted floral work. Lu-Ray collectors have adopted the word "chocolate" when talking about the first, straight sided demitasse set.

The coffeepot on the left is the original. Commonly called the "chocolate pot" or "straight sided" pot, it was replaced by the A.D. pot (shown in blue on the right) in 1939, only a year after Lu-Ray was introduced. The chocolate pot is much harder to find than the A.D. pot. Both come in the first four colors only.

VALUES: (4 original colors)
chocolate pot - $700-850
A.D. coffee pot - $200-225

Here is a comparison shot of three sugars found in Lu-Ray. To the left is the regular sugar. It is the Empire shape sugar and comes in all five colors.

To the far right is the chocolate sugar. It was in production for the first year and is very hard to find today. They come in the first four colors only.

In the middle is the individual (A.D.) sugar which replaced the chocolate sugar in 1939. It was discontinued before 1948 and doesn't come in gray.

VALUES:	4 original colors	gray
regular sugar	$18-20	$65-75
A.D. sugar	$60-80	___
chocolate sugar	$400-500	___

Chocolate or straight sided sugars in blue and pink. Of the four styles of sugars found in Lu-Ray, this type is the rarest. They come in the first four colors only and were produced until they were replaced by the A.D. sugar in early 1940. See table above for values.

Unhandled or "handle-less" sugars come in four colors only. These are usually found in Versatile sets in pastel colors with decal and bronze treatments from the late 1950s (see Versatile Pastel section.) In the Lu-Ray line, they no doubt replaced the older Empire shape sugar. Since they come from the end of Lu-Ray's production, expect to be unmarked. Recently a handleless sugar was found in the turquoise glaze from Pebbleford.

One interesting thing to note, the lids to these sugars are identical to the teapot lid with the exception that the sugar lid lacks a large flange.

VALUES: 4 original colors - $35-40

To the left is the regular creamer in gray. It is from the Empire shape and comes in all five colors. It was made for the entire production run of Lu-Ray.

To the far right in blue is the chocolate creamer. It was made for the first year only and was replaced by the individual creamer in 1939.

The individual creamer (A.D. creamer) comes in the first five colors only. It is a smaller version of the regular creamer.

VALUES:	4 original colors	gray
regular creamer	$8-10	$40-50
A.D. creamer	$30-40	____
chocolate creamer	$350-450	____

Chocolate set creamers in blue, pink and green. Also known as "straight-sided" creamers, they are very hard to find and come in the first four colors only.

On the left is the sauceboat fixed stand; to the right is the regular sauceboat. Though they were part of the original Lu-Ray line, the fixed stand had the longest continous production. It can be found in all five Lu-Ray colors, with gray being the hardest to find.

The regular sauceboat was discontinued sometime before 1947. As a result, the sauceboat does not come in gray. In the mid 50s the sauceboat was brought back to be used with various Versatile shapes in pastel glazes. For more on the sauceboat being used with Versatile, see section on Versatile Pastels.

VALUES: regular sauceboat: 4 original colors - $20-25
gravy fast stand: 4 original colors - $35-40
gravy fast stand: gray - $75+

The Empire shape shakers were available for Lu-Ray's entire production run. They come in all five colors as shown. You will be able to tell the difference between the salt and the pepper based on the size of the holes. For the most part, the shakers are marked "USA."

VALUES: Per pair
4 orig. colors - $15-20
gray - $40-45

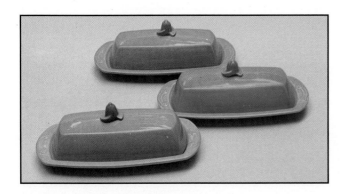

Shown in gray, pink and blue, the butter dish comes in all five colors.

VALUES: 4 original colors - $55-65
gray - $150-175

In case you find an unmarked example, you will be able to identify the base as being Lu-Ray by the Laurel type tab handle ornamentation.

Neither of the two styles of water jugs were available in gray. The yellow footed example on the right was introduced in early 1939 as an "ice-lip jug" and was later replaced by the flat bottom blue version on the left. Except for the foot, they are basically identical. They come in the first four colors only.

VALUES: 4 original colors
footed jug - $125-150
flat bottom jug - $80-95

The juice pitcher was added to the line in early 1941. It is much harder to find than its larger water jug counterpart. Shown with the juice pitcher are the juice tumblers. In the Feb. 1941 issue of *China, Glass and Lamps*, the tumbler is listed as a "grapefruit tumbler." It stands 3¼" tall. The juice tumblers and juice pitcher were never made in gray.

VALUES: Pitcher - 4 original colors - $150-175

Here are the only two sizes of tumblers found in Lu-Ray: the juice tumblers (foreground) and Water tumblers (background). Water tumblers stand 4¼". Juice tumblers are 1" smaller at 3¼". Both styles come in the colors shown − no gray.

VALUES: 4 original colors: either style - $65-75

There are two styles of teapots in Lu-Ray. To the right is the first type, called "flat spout" since the spout extends straight forward and flat from the body. The flat spout teapot comes in the first four colors only.

The gray teapot on the left is called a "curved spout" teapot for obvious reasons. It comes in all five Lu-Ray colors. Both have the same

capacities and have lids which are identical in both shape and dimension.

Note the angles on the top of the handles for each teapot. The curved spout teapot's handle points upward, whereas the flat spout teapot's handle is slightly flatter.

VALUES: flat spout: 4 original colors - $125-150
curved spout: 4 original colors - $85-95   gray - $400-500

The casserole was discontinued sometime before gray became a color in 1948. It, like the sauce boat, would be brought back in several late Versatile lines in pastel glazes. (see section on Versatile Pastels.)

VALUES: 4 original colors - $100-125

According to Mr. Smith, these coasters were used as give away's or salesmen's samples. They were made a part of the line in 1942 and come in the first four colors only. These have a "dish" or bowl shape – not at all flat like a traditional coaster. Sometimes dealers will label these as ashtrays or nut dishes. They have a diameter of 41/2".

VALUES: 4 original colors - $90-100

These small coasters are often misidentified as Lu-Ray. Eight of these was found with the original box which read: JERYWIL PRODUCTS. They come in Lu-Ray like pastel shades of blue, green and yellow. The fourth color is a light beige.

All three vases are rare and command high prices. In the center is the Epergne (pronounced: "ah-purn"). It is listed in the February 1939 edition of *China, Glass and Lamps* as, ". . . a double centerpiece of vase and bowl . . ." Standing 81/2" tall and having a base diameter of 9", it is a rather large and unusual piece to belong to a line of dinnerware. In the center, there is a ring of holes which act as a flower frog.

This piece was made in two parts: the bowl and the stem. As soon as they were taken out of the mold cast, they were attached and fired.

To the left is a small bud urn. It stands only 31/2" tall.

On the right, in yellow, is a the bud vase. Standing 33/4", it is only slightly taller than the bud urn.

All three sizes were discontinued during the mid 40s and,

as a result, can not be found in gray.

VALUES: 4 original colors: any style - $250-275

Muffin covers on 8" plates. Surprisingly, the covers and the plates were sold separately. While the 8" plate was already in production, the cover was not introduced until 1940. Since the cover was discontinued before the advent of gray, you will find them in the first four colors only. They have a base diameter of 6¼".

VALUES: 4 original colors - $95-105

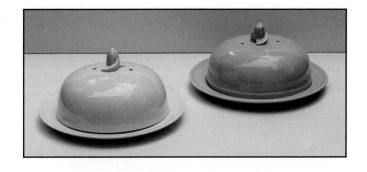

The double egg cup was produced specifically for Lu-Ray. It would later be used with the Pebbleford line, so don't be surprised to find this shape in speckled glazes. Shown are Lu-Ray egg cups in all five glazes. Gray egg cups are hard to find, but the other four colors are somewhat easy to find. The large cup has a diameter of 3½" the smaller cup, which has a dry foot ring, has a diameter of 2".

VALUES: 4 original colors - $24-28
                gray - $65-75

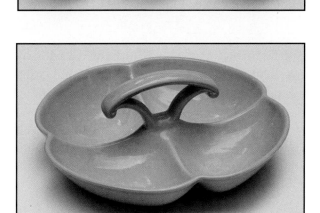

This is the one-piece four-section relish tray in blue. They come in the first four colors only.

VALUES: 4 original colors - $90-110

The cake lifter is a shape that was made by both TS & T and its neighbor pottery, Harker. It is generally found in white with decal treatments along with a matching TS & T. If you are unsure yours is the Harker/TS & T version, look for three lines which cross the handle. Also, towards the hole is a triangular wedge shape indention.

Shown along with the cake lifter is an Ever Yours creamer in Persian Cream. Almost every TS & T shape made in the late 30s, 40s and 50s has an example found in Lu-Ray glazes, especially Conversation, Versatile and Vogue. These are discussed in the next section.

VALUES:
TS&T/Harker cake lifter, Lu-Ray glazes - $20-25
Ever Yours creamer, Lu-Ray glazes - $8

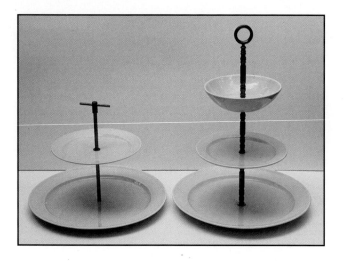

Tid bit trays. There are several variations of trays which were assembled at the TS & T plant. To the left is an unusual example in gray with a cross handle. The green three-tired tray uses a Versatile shape fruit cup for the top piece. Trays with the round handle are the most common. Not only were Lu-Ray pieces used, but so were Versatile, Pebbleford, and Conversation.

Sometimes odd lids can be found. Coffeepot and teapot lids will always have a large flange to securely fit the base. Here is a breakdown of the lids with diameters.

Coffeepot lids: A.D. Pot - $2^{1/2}$"

                     Chocolate Pot - $2^{7/8}$"

Sugar lids: Regular - 3"

                     A.D. sugar - 2"

                     Chocolate sugar - $2^{5/8}$"

                     handleless sugar - 4"

Teapot lids: 4"

Casserole lids: $8^{1/4}$"

Mr. Smith explained that there were several trial glazes under consideration in the 1940s. Here are two of those glazes which have recently been found on the open market.

Shown on the left is a Lu-Ray plate in the standard gray glaze. On the right is a marked Lu-Ray plate in a charcoal gray glaze.

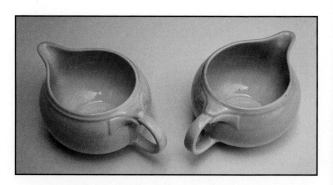

To the left is a yellow Lu-Ray creamer. On the right is another trial glaze – this time, a very light chartreuse. The chartreuse is so light that it could easily be confused as yellow. The raised portions around the handle reviles the yellow-green color much better than the rest of the body.

Lu-Ray with Treatments

The following Lu-Ray items all have treatments. In general, they can go for 2 times to 4 times the normal cost of regular untreated pieces, especially when marked Lu-Ray.

You will find TS & T calendar plates on both Lu-Ray and Pebbleford blanks. Here are three on Lu-Ray with the center design of a Dutch windmill. The larger 10" plate in the background has gold filigree work around the rim. Calendar plates have been found for the years 1958 through 1962 inclusive.

In the early 1950s, gray Lu-Ray was the basis for five decaled dinnerware lines as well as several striped patterns. An example of each decal treatment is shown. Most of these decals can be found on another TS & T 50s shape, Conversation.

The creamer on the far left has a rose decal. Homer Laughlin collectors should recognize this decal since HLC used it on several shapes including Rhythm, Virginia Rose and Kitchen Kraft. The rose treatment was also used by Cannonsburg Pottery.

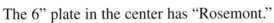

The 6" plate in the center has "Rosemont."
The platter has a large treatment of violets called, "Marsh Violet".
"Sea Shells" is the name of the treatment on the cup and saucer.
Finally, "Coffee Tree" appears on the fruit cup.

Because of the handleless sugar, this group probably comes from the late 1950s. The treatment is called, "Mardi Gras" and is very popular with collectors. You will find other pieces than those shown.

Vases in gold trim.

A.D. coffeepot and tumbler with Colonial
couple decal treatments and gold trim.

Empire shapes in an
iridescent glaze with gold trim.

A.D. cup and saucer in white
with pine cone treatment.

A.D. cup and saucer in Surf Green with
rose and gold trim.

A.D. cup and saucer in Persian Cream
with 50s decal and gold trim.

A.D. cup and saucer originally in
Sharon Pink decorated in gold.

"601" pink cake plate with handle.
601 is a pattern name referring
to the silver/platinum
bands running along the rim.

Non Lu-Ray Pastels

TS & T used about 20 different shapes for dinnerware lines. Empire and Laurel have already been discussed as being part of the Lu-Ray line, but there were three other TS & T shapes which were dipped in the Lu-Ray glazes. They are: Vogue, Conversation, Versatile. The Plymouth shape was also given the Lu-Ray glazes and sold as "Interstate Sunrise Ware," but these pieces are rare.

Vogue Pastels

Vogue was a shape used by TS & T in the 1930s and very early 40s. Handles have a floral ornamentation at the top, similar to Vistosa's, and flat pieces have a repeated "teardrop" or paisley design. Found more often with decal treatments, Vogue items were given Lu-Ray colors and sold through Montgomery Ward's in the early 1940s. Though Vogue was the primary shape used, the name given to the line was, "Rainbow." The following is a listing of the items which were available:

10" plate	6" plate	sugar	creamer	lug soup	platter
teacup	saucer	gravy	teapot	jug	shakers

The jug and shakers were not Vogue pieces but were the Empire shapes, which were used in the standard Lu-Ray line.

Of the very few Vogue Pastel items I have seen, none have been marked. They are available in the four colors of: Sharon Pink, Windsor Blue, Persian Cream, and Surf Green. It is unlikely this was a big seller in its day since very little is found now.

Values are given for any color. (Note: Vogue items with decal treatments are worth considerably less.)

Vogue Pastels Dinner Plates
VALUES: $10-15

Vogue Pastels 6" plates.
VALUES: $6-8

Vogue Pastels cups and saucers.
VALUES: Cups - $10-12   Saucers - $4-6

Vogue Pastels sugar (without lid) and creamer.
VALUES: sugar with lid - $20-25

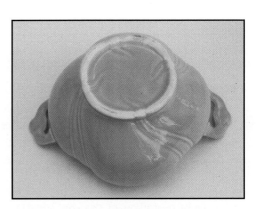

Hollowware items like this sugar as well
as the creamer and teapot have swirl
modeling that continues from the front
on the body to the underside.

Vogue creamers in
Windsor Blue and Sharon Pink.
VALUES: $8-12

Vogue teapot in Sharon Pink.
VALUES: $50-60

Vogue fruit cups in all four Lu-Ray colors.
VALUES: $6-8

Vogue lug soup in Sharon Pink.
VALUES: $8-12

Vogue gravy fast stands in
Windsor Blue and Sharon Pink.
VALUES: $25-30

Vogue platter in surf green.
VALUES: $15-18

Conversation Pastels

Conversation is a rectangular/square shape with slightly rounded edges. It was designed by Walter D. Teague and was produced from 1950 until just before 1955. Though made for only 6 years, Conversation with decal treatments or solid colors is very easy to find.

Conversation in pastel glazes is a rather limited line and so far, none of the more exotic pieces such as coffee pots, casseroles, or water jugs have been found in the LuRay colors. Simple items such as plates, platters, serving bowls, cups, saucers, creamers and covered sugars are all that have been discovered thus far.

Within a four month period, I was able to assemble 70 pieces of Conversation Pastels from both antique shops and eBay. There should be no trouble for the collector who wants to put together a set. The backstamps of my pieces run from late 1950 until late 1953.

Conversation in pastel glazes was made by TS & T for Montgomery Wards in the early 50s in the colors gray, blue, pink and yellow. It seems that Surf Green, while a standard Lu-Ray color, was not used in Conversation until gray was discontinued by 1953 and when a replacement color was needed. Since the entire line of Conversation was discontinued shortly thereafter, Surf Green Conversation items should be the most difficult to locate.

Chips on the underside are what to look out for with this line. In general, the glazes are clean and even with no crazing or runs.

Values are given for Chatham gray, Windsor Blue, Sharon Pink and Persian Cream (yellow).
Double values for any item found in Surf Green.

10" Conversation dinner plates.
VALUES: $10-12

6" plates in pink, gray,
yellow and green.
VALUES: $6-8

Stack of Conversation 5 1/2" fruit cups
in all five Lu-Ray pastel colors.
VALUES: $7.50-9.50

Pair of 6 1/2" Oatmeal bowls in pink and blue.
VALUES: $8-10

9" nappy in blue.
VALUES: $12-15

Oval baker in pink.
VALUES: $12-15

Platters: large 13 1/2" x 10";
medium 11" x 8".
VALUES: $10-12

Cups and saucers in all five Lu-Ray colors.
VALUES: Cups - $5-8
Saucers - $2-4

Covered sugars in pink and yellow.
VALUES: with lid - $12-15

Creamers in blue, pink and yellow.
VALUES: $5-8

Sauceboat in yellow with a blue stand
that measures 8 1/2" x 5 1/4".
VALUES: Sauceboat - $8-12
Stand (hard to find) - $12-15

Versatile is a 50s line by TS & T which comes in several forms. First of all, the flatware (plates, platters, saucers, small bowls) are all the same for each Versatile line. One version is called FORMAL which includes hollowware with pedestal bases and flared finials. The second is called INFORMAL and is used with the Pebbleford line discussed in a different section in this book. Informal Versatile is a casual line − meant to be used for outdoor barbecues or at the dining room table.

Most of the Versatile pieces found in Lu-Ray glazes are flatware so they could belong to either the Formal or Informal version. In many cases, the Versatile pastel items are mixed with unmarked Lu-Ray creamers, handleless sugars, sauceboats and shakers.

Values are given for any color.

This Versatile marking can be found on most flat pieces such as plates, saucers and platters. Cups, sugars and other hollowware pieces are generally unmarked.

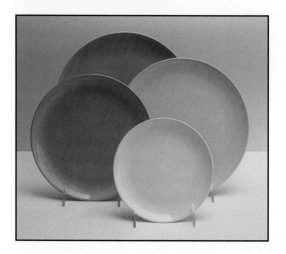

Versatile Pastels 10", 8" and 6" plates in pink, green, blue and yellow. The blue pastel glaze found on the Versatile shape is ever so slightly darker than the Windsor Blue used in Lu-Ray. The other three colors are the same as those used in Lu-Ray; Surf Green, Persian Cream, and Sharon Pink.

VALUES: 10" plate - $6-8
                 8" plate - $5-7
                 6" plate - $3-4

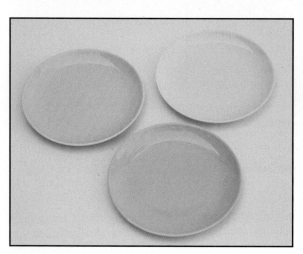

Versatile Pastels 6" plates.

Versatile cups and saucers. These have an Empire body without a turned foot and a restyled handle.

VALUES: cups - $4-6
saucers - $2-3

Versatile round serving bowl in Sharon Pink.

VALUES: $8-10

Versatile oval serving bowls; yellow and green.

VALUES: $8-10

Versatile Pastels small bowls. The green bowl in the background has a diameter of 6¾". The other three measure 5¼" across.

VALUES: 6¾" bowl - $5-7
5¼" bowl - $4-6

Versatile 11 1/2" platter in Surf Green.

VALUES: $7-9

Versatile 13" platter with the Dwarf Pine treatment. Generally, the Dwarf Pine decal is found on pink Formal Versatile. Not only is it unusual to see the treatment on a yellow piece of Versatile, but with a furniture advertisement from South Carolina. Dwarf Pine decals with advertisements can also be found on Lu-Ray platters.

VALUES:

    Dwarf Pine with ad. on Versatile - $10-15

    Dwarf Pine with ad. on Lu-Ray - $20-25

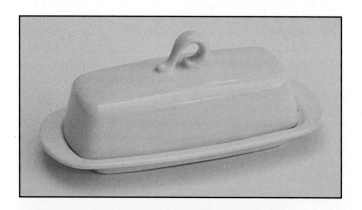

Informal Versatile covered butter in Persian Cream.

VALUES: $10-12

Formal Versatile covered casserole in Sharon Pink. Notice the foot, finial and overall formal look to this casserole.

VALUES: $20-25

Handleless sugar with unusual lid.

VALUES: $10-12

There are several lines which are combinations of the Versatile shapes with the Empire/Lu-Ray hollowware. The first of these mixed lines is called, "Sugar and Spice". The shapes are in Lu-Ray's surf green glaze and are given a bronze trim. Most of the Versatile pieces found in these sets are marked and have been found with date codes ranging from 1954 to 1959. Plates in all sizes, cups, saucers and bowls are very easy to find.

Sugar and Spice plates in the 10", 8" and 6" sizes. In the foreground is the cup and saucer.

Sugar and Spice 13" platter, lug soup and handleless sugars. Note the two variations of lids. The sugar in front has a Versatile shape lid; the handleless sugar in back has the Empire/Lu-Ray finial.

Sugar and Spice creamer, round serving bowl and fruit cup.

Sugar and Spice gravyboat, teapot and shakers.

Here are two styles of cups. The one on the left is an Empire shape cup. It has a little circle at the inner top part of the handle. Ordinarily Empire cups have a hand turned foot, but examples found in Sugar and Spice have blunt feet. To the right is a restyled cup, sometimes called the "casual" type Versatile cup. It is identical to the Empire cup except the small circle inside the handle has been removed.

TS & T made another line similiar to Sugar and Spice in the 50s. This time Persian Cream was used with the bronze trim. "Honey and Butter" is the name of this line and is harder to find than Sugar and Spice.

Honey and Butter creamer, handleless sugar without lid, shakers and covered casserole.

Honey and Butter fruit cup, oval baker, and sauceboat.

This unusual cream and sugar is similar to Honey and Butter, but it has a blue/gray trim in combination with the bronze.

VALUES: Persian Cream with
blue/bronze trim:
sugar with lid - $25+
creamer - $18-20

The following values are for the items found in Sugar and Spice and Honey and Butter treatments.

Versatile shapes:

10" plate -	$8-10
8" plate -	$8-10
6" plate -	$5-7
lug soup -	$8-10
cup (either style) - $6-8	
13" platter -	$10-12
fruit cup -	$5-7
round serving bowl -	$8-10
oval serving bowl -	$10-12
saucer -	$4-5
handleless sugar,	
Versatile lid -	$12-15

Empire/Lu-Ray shapes:

sauceboat -	$12-15
creamer -	$10-12
shakers, pr. -	$15+
teapot -	$20-25
casserole -	$25-30
handleless sugar,	
Lu-Ray type lid-	$12-15

Leaf Fantasy Snack Set

The leaf snack sets consist of a cup and a leaf plate with an indentation for the cup. These sets were made in solid colors by both Universal Pottery and Taylor, Smith and Taylor. The TS & T versions come in the Lu-Ray pastel colors whereas Universal's come in peach, green, yellow and gray.

The leaf plate measures 10" at its longest point. The general marking found on TS & T's leaf plate is: Leaf Fantasy BY Taylor Smith Taylor, U.S.A. One was recently found with a Lu-Ray backstamp.

Yellow, green, pink and gray seem to be the standard colors for the Leaf Fantasy sets.

VALUES: TS & T Leaf Plate (any color) - $15
TS & T Leaf Cup (any color) - $20

Pebbleford is a 1950s dinnerware line. Designed by John Gilkes, it was produced by Taylor, Smith and Taylor from 1953 until 1960 using the Informal Versatile shape. Most 50s dinnerware lines consist of clean streamline shapes that are not cluttered with decoration or ornamentation. They are free form and flowing lacking the "harshness" of Fiesta and other Art Deco lines of the previous two decades.

The colored glazes used in Pebbleford contain iron fillings which produce an all-over speckled effect. The color assortment underwent changes during the 7 year production of Pebbleford. It started out with sunburst (a yellow-chartreuse), turquoise, pink, and granite (a light gray). In 1956, marble (white) and Teal (which is more of a dark green than teal) was added and granite was replaced by mint green. Late additions of Honey, Sand and Burnt Orange complete the standard colors.

There is one final color to be mentioned which is not found in any price lists or documents: an unnamed green. This color, which is very similar to mint green has appeared on a number of Ever Yours pieces.

You will find four sizes of plates in the Pebbleford line: the bread and butter plate - 6", the salad plate - 7", the dinner plate - 10", and the chop plate - 12". Shown in the image is the dinner plate in mint green and a 6"plate in pink.

VALUES: 12" plate - $12-15   7" plate - $5-8
10" plate - $8-10   6" plate - $3-5

Pebbleford 10" calendar plate.

VALUES: any year - $12-15

Platters are somewhat easy to find in all the Pebbleford colors. Shown in turquoise, they measure 13" and 11".

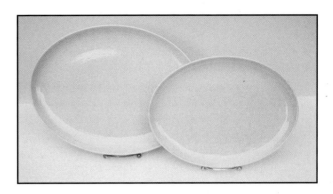

VALUES: 11" Platter - $10-12
                13" Platter - $12-15

Here is the cup and saucer in Sand. Although there are several forms of Versatile cups, the only ones used for Pebbleford are the Informal version.

VALUES: cup - $5-8   saucer - $3-5

There are two types of sugar bowls in the Pebbleford line. In pink is the version with no handles on the base. The other style with base handles is in Teal. What collectors may find surprising is that these two versions were offered at the same time. It would seem natural that one replaced the other during production, but price lists indicate that was not the case.

VALUES: covered sugar with base handles - $8-10
                covered sugar without base handles - $10-12

The sauceboat in mint green with a Sand creamer.

VALUES:
    sauceboat - $12-15
    creamer - $6-8

Syrup pitcher in Sunburst.
VALUE: $15-18

These shakers are very similar in design to the syrup and have been found in many Pebbleford colors. The salt and pepper differ in heights. Both the shakers and the "syrup" are Ever Yours shapes. **VALUES:** $15-20 a pair

These are the more common regular Pebbleford shakers in Sand.
VALUE: $10-12 a pair

The divided baker in pink.
VALUE: $15-20

Oval vegetable in Sand.
VALUES: $10-12

To the left is a round serving bowl in Sunburst and to the right is a coupe soup in teal.

VALUES: serving bowl - $10-12
coupe soup - $6-9

The pickle in sunburst and fruit cup in burnt orange.

VALUES: pickle - $8-10 fruit cup - $6-8

Very few sets of Lu-Ray mixing bowls have been found in Pebbleford glazes. It was recently learned that they were produced for only one year. Shown here is the 10 1/4" size in Sunburst and the 7" size in Granite.

The other two Pebbleford mixing bowls: 8 3/4" in Sand and 5 1/2" in Teal.

VALUES: any size, any color - $65-75

The covered casserole in Sunburst.

VALUES: $30-35

Shown here in Granite is the lug soup with a hard to find lid.

VALUES: lug soup base - $6-9
lug soup lid - $12-15

The egg cups, which were originally designed for Lu-Ray, in the Pebbleford glazes of Teal and Sunburst.

VALUES: $12-15

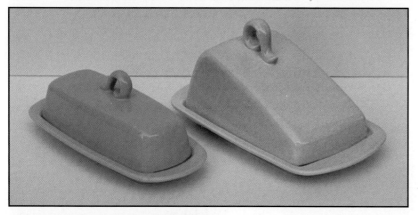

The covered butter in pink and a covered cheese dish in Sunburst. All of the cheese dishes that have been found thus far have been in Sunburst.

VALUES: covered butter - $15-18
covered cheese - $50-60

Water Jug in turquoise.
VALUES: $20-25

Covered teapot in granite.
VALUES: $30-35

Here are the two styles of Pebbleford coffeepots. The one on the left in Sand has a base opening of 3" whereas the Sunburst on the right has an opening of 4".

VALUES: coffeepot, either style - $25-30

Shown in Pebbleford pink and turquoise glazes is the *Formal* style coffeepot. At least another pink one has been found as well as two in an unnamed green glaze.

VALUES: Formal style coffeepot in standard
Pebbleford colors - $40-45

These two items, the Formal style coffeepot and the syrup are in an unnamed green glaze – a glaze primarily found on Ever Yours shapes. They are not in mint green, but the color is very close. Notice the syrup is two-toned with a turquoise interior.

VALUES: Formal Style Coffeepot in
unnamed green - $60+

To the left is a Sand sauceboat and to the right an unusual shaped bowl in the Honey glaze. These two colors are very similar and even when side-by-side in person, the difference is hard to tell. Honey is slightly brighter and golden in comparison to sand and is used with Reveille – a line which features a rooster decal.

VALUES: sauceboat - $12-15   flared bowl - $20-25

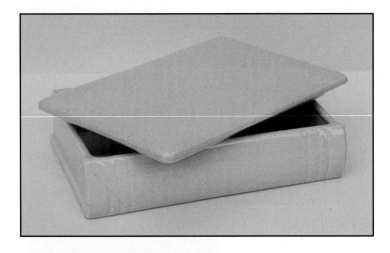

Marked Pebbleford is this unique covered box in the shape of a book. The owner speculates that its a cigarette or cigar holder. The backstamp has a date code of 1954.

VALUES: $85+

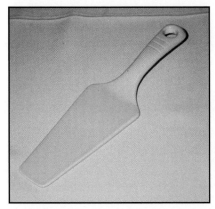

This is the TS & T/Harker cake lifter in the Pebbleford glaze, turquoise. These can also be found in Lu-Ray glazes as well as with decal treatments with TS & T cake plates.

VALUES: $20-25

Ever Yours, a shape meant for decal treatments, was designed by Gilkes and was produced from 1958 until 1965. The body of the ware was much heavier than the Versatile shapes with thick streamline rims.

In the past year ther have been several items in the Ever Yours shape that have appeared in Pebbleford glazes. Ever Yours flat pieces such as plates, platters and saucers all come from the Versatile line. These pieces in conjunction with Ever Yours sugars, creamers and cups, all in Pebbleford glazes, could constitute a set, but there is a lack of evidence to make the claim that the Ever Yours shape in Pebbleford glazes was ever marketed.

Not shown is an Ever Yours carafe. One was recently found in the pink Pebbleford glaze.

VALUES: $20-25

Here are a collection of Ever Yours teacups and (Versatile shape) saucers in Pebbleford colors: unnamed green, sunburst, pink and turquoise.

VALUES: Ever Yours cups in Pebbleford glases - $8-10

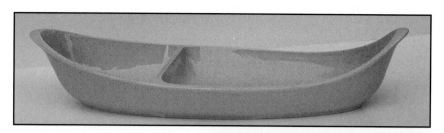

The Ever Yours divided pickle in turquoise.

VALUES: $12-15

At least two Ever Yours covered sugars in Pebbleford glazes have been discovered thus far. Shown with a white lid is the Ever Yours sugar in pink. The other has both the base and the lid in Sunburst.

VALUES: Every Yours sugars
               base and lid same color - $10-12
               base in Pebbleford glaze/white lid - $8-10

Ever Yours creamers in Sunburst and pink.

VALUES: $8-10

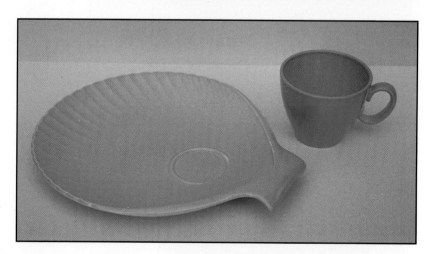

A dozen of these sets were found in the Chester/East Liverpool area. They are made up of a shell plate (not belonging to any particular TS & T line) and an Ever Yours teacup all in Pebbleford pink. A company memo dated December 1, 1965 sheds some light on these sets:

TAYLOR TREATS

Composition: 4 shell plates and 4 cups packed in strawless carton. Patter is to be designated. They will be done in Pebbleford colors and can be packed solid (one color only) *or rainbow* (mixed colors). *They will be done in ivory using a Catalina cup with either silver or gold line* (trim).

Prices were given as $2.80 for a set of four in either Pebbleford or Ivory with trim. It is interesting to note that the Pebbleford glazes were still being used well into 1965.

VALUES: shell plates in Pebbleford glazes - $20-25 each

Vistosa, in its bold colors of red, cobalt, green and yellow, was introduced in 1938 by Taylor Smith and Taylor.

In the late '30s, many potteries were producing dinnerware shapes with the Art Deco/Streamline form. Vistosa is a departure from the rigid geometric theme with its pie crust edging and smooth bulbous surfaces. The small floral sculpting, which is reminiscent of Vogue, another TS & T shape, can be found on the lug handles of the round platters, the handles on the ball jug, teapot, sauceboat, sugar and creamer.

The colors are bold yet at the same time, they are soft with a matte finish. Here again TS & T departs from the norm as many other solid colored dinnerware lines of the day had a very hard and glossy feel.

Vistosa is one of the more difficult lines to locate and for the past several years, the prices have risen dramatically. The ball jug which had an estimated value of about $40 in 1995 now goes for over $100. Some pieces such as the sauce boat and the large footed salad bowl are virtually impossible to find and are valued at well over $100 each. But, when Vistosa is found, it is generally marked with an inkstamp though some items have an incised marking. No other line like Vistosa has been made so confusing it with another solid colored dinnerware shouldn't happen.

On very rare occasions, Vistosa can be found with decal treatments.

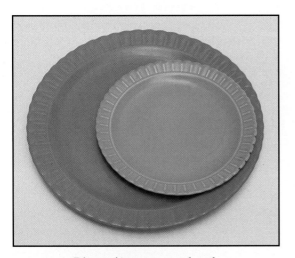

Plates in green and red.

Regular cups and saucers.

Lug platter

Lug soup bowl and fruit cup.

Ball jug in red.

Creamer and sugar.

Here are two unusual Vistosa pieces. The ball jug is in Windsor Blue. Though this was a standard color in Lu-Ray, it was never intended to be used with Vistosa. Obviously this jug was made by a TS & T employee.

The shakers are in a very strange brown-matte glaze. Mr. Smith examined these and was able to provide an explanation. He said that when they were experimenting with red colored glazes, many were unstable and difficult to use. These shakers were originally glazed in one of the prototype red colors. When they were fired, the red coloring burned away leaving a brown residue.

VALUES: Vistosa items

10" plate	$40-45	fruit cup	$10-12
9" plate	$12-15	coupe soup	$15-18
7" plate	$8-10	lug soup	$20-25
6" plate	$5-7	round serving bowl	$55-50
11" lug round platter	$30-35	footed salad bowl	$250+
14" lug round platter	$52-58	creamer	$20-25
tea cup	$12-15	sugar	$38-42
saucer	$3-4	gravy	$250+
A.D. cup	$25-30	ball jug	$85-110
A.D. saucer	$18-20	teapot	$100-125
egg cup	$45-50	shakers, pr.	$15-20

Knowels Line: Yorktown

Yorktown by the Edwin M. Knowles China Company of Newell, WV was released about the same time as Fiesta in 1936, following suit of the surrounding potteries such as Homer Laughlin and Taylor, Smith and Taylor among others. Yorktown can be distinguished by the swept design of finials, handles, and tab extensions on flat pieces. This unique feature that is not typical on other colorware.

Yorktown shape with anniversary logo that reads: EAST LIVERPOOL, 1886-1936 JUNE 1-2-3. This coaster measures 4¾" from tab to tab. Many Yorktown items can be found with red and/or blue trim.

Colors are diverse in this line: yellow, red, maroon, cadet (medium blue), green, cobalt, pink, and rust. There are also a wide variety of decaled lines using the Yorktown shape.

Prices have been rising for this line due to its growing popularity. As Fiesta and LuRay become more and more expensive, the beginning collector will generally seek out something affordable like Yorktown and other lesser known lines in this chapter. There are some unusual pieces to this line such as the candleholders, which I have yet to see in a solid color. Prices are given along with the Deanna line and are for any color.

A large shallow bowl, or console bowl (10½" x 2¼") in cobalt. Most potters marked the ware before applying a glaze. With cobalt items, it is almost impossible to see the marking if any exists. It would be very easy for a beginner or uneducated dealer to confuse an item like this for Fiesta.

A burgundy teacup and saucer.

Light green covered sugar and covered casserole in yellow.

Medium blue creamer.

Close up of a medium blue fruit cup
on a yellow 6" plate.

10" plate in rust, 9" plate in red, oatmeal bowl in yellow, fruit cup in medium blue, 6" plate in yellow.

Knowels Lines: Deanna

Another Knowles colorware line, Deanna, was introduced in the late 30s. Like Yorktown, Deanna can be found with both decal treatments and solid colors. Deanna's claim to fame is being divided into two distinct color lines; a practice not common with potteries in the Ohio River Valley area. The colors for the first line are bold green, blue, red and yellow which are similar to Fiesta's colors. The second line is called Caribbean. Pastel shades of Powder Blue, Lemon Yellow, Peach (Buff) and Turquoise make up this line. Colors which were added later were maroon, pink and rust which are more common in Yorktown than Deanna.

Pastel shades are more common than the bold colors. It is up to the individual collector whether he or she wishes to mix the two tones together.

The decoration on Deanna shapes is simple: three raised rings along the rim. This theme is repeated on handles and finials. Knowles was very good about marking their products which eliminates doubt when encountering pieces in shops or flea markets.

Small Deanna shape promotional coaster which reads:

THIS IS YOUR INVITATION TO VISIT OUR DISPLAY AT THE HOME FURNISHINGS BUILDING, NEW YORK WORLD'S FAIR, 1939. EDWIN M. KNOWLES CHINA CO., EAST LIVERPOOL, OHIO.

Creamer in red and covered sugar in pink.

Dinner plates in pink and maroon.

Fruit cup in lemon yellow.

8" round serving bowl
in the pastel glaze, turquoise.

Cups and saucers in yellow and green.

Yorktown and Deanna items
VALUES: any color
(items with "*" are from the Yorktown line only)

10" plate	$8-10	creamer	$8-10
9" plate	$6-8	cov. sugar	$12-15
8" plate	$8-10	shakers, pr.	$12-15
7" plate	$4-5	teapot	$30-35
6" plate	$3-4	cup	$6-8
15" platter	$12-15	saucer	$1-2
13" platter	$10-12	A.D. cup	$10-12
11" platter	$10-12	A.D. saucer	$4-6
fruit (5") cup	$5-6	gravyboat	$12-15
lug soup	$8-10	coaster	$10-12
coupe soup	$7-9	*candleholders	$85+
36s bowl	$10-12	covd. casserole	$20-25
*console bowl	$15-18		
oatmeal (6") bowl	$7-9		

Accent

This typically styled 1950s dinnerware was produced by Knowles.

Like 1950s lines such as Ballerina and Rhythm, Accent is made up of a plain rounded uncluttered shapes. The tab soup bowls and stubby shakers are rather unique, but the flat ware and berry bowls could be mixed with other lines and it would be very hard to notice the difference.

Brown is seldom seen in colored dinnerware lines. It along with chartreuse, gray and dark green make up the known colors of this line. Because this line is not well known, while hard to find, values are very low due to lack of demand. Prices are for any color. In some vintage ads, white was offered as a "contrasting color." "Sunset Glazes" is the Accent shape in pastel colors.

The flat pieces will have a Knowles marking with a K in an oval similar to the marking found on the advertising piece shown in the image.

At the left is a creamer in chartreuse, on the right is a covered sugar in dark green.

VALUES: creamer - $4-5

covd. sugar - $6-8

Stubby shakers in dark green.

VALUES: $6-8 a pair

Serving bowl in brown.

VALUES: $4-5

Tea cups and saucers in the known colors: brown, dark green, gray and chartreuse.

VALUES: cup - $3-4

saucer - $1

11" oval platter in gray.

VALUES: $6-8

Shown on the left are tab handled soups. On the right are fruit cups.

VALUES: tab soups - $6-8
fruit cup - $3-4

10" dinner plate with 6" plate.
VALUES: 10" plate - $5-8
6" plate - $4-5

Snack set in chartreuse.
VALUES: snack plate - $8-10
cup (same as teacup) - $3-4

Mt. Clemens Lines: Petal

Petal was made by the Mt. Clemens Pottery Company in Mt. Clemens, Michigan. The shape is called Toulon and can be found with decal treatments. Maroon and green are the easiest colors to find and are generally darker than similar colors made by other companies. Yellow is virtually impossible to locate. In between lies blue which, in my opinion, is the best shade of blue produced by any pottery. This distinctive color is brighter than new Fiesta's sapphire.

Once in a while a piece can be found with the Mt. Clemens' backstamp. Teacups have a raised USA mold mark but, more often than not, items from this line are unmarked.

The name Petal is sometimes incorrectly applied to Georgette by W.S. George (see section of same title).

It would be easy to assemble a service for four in green and maroon since place setting items in those colors are very common.

In maroon: a teacup which is marked "USA" in the mold, a fruit cup, and a dinner plate. A 7" plate in the beautiful blue glaze.

6" plate in maroon, and a dinner plate in green, teacup in blue.

Covered butter in green.

Round serving bowl, 8½" in diameter, in the uncommon rich blue glaze.

The A.D. sugar and creamer shown in the deep blue glaze has the same raised mold markings as the teacups. These have paneled sides, but lack the general petal design. Petal has curved handles but the A.D. sugar and creamer have flat-top handles. The A.D. sugar and creamer were general shapes used by Mt. Clemens and were dipped in the colored glazes. They have been found in blue, green and maroon as well as with decal treatments.

Same AD creamer and sugar set, this time in maroon.

Two sizes of platters: 11" and 9" along with a sauce boat in yellow. Sauceboats have a raised USA marking.

Creamer and sugar in green. Both of these items are usually found unmarked.

The round serving bowl in a hard to find pink glaze. This particular bowl was found with the MCPCo inkstamp.

Covered casserole in green.

PETAL VALUES: Two prices are given for each piece of Petal:
low - maroon and green
high - any other color

9" plate -	$8 - 15	casserole -	$20 - 30+
7" plate -	$7 - 12	creamer -	$ 8 - 15
6" plate -	$6 - 10	A.D. creamer -	$ 6 - 12
9" platter -	$8 - 15	cov. sugar -	$10 - 20
11" platter -	$8 - 15	A.D. sugar -	$ 6 - 12
cup -	$7 - 12	gravyboat -	$10 - 15
saucer -	$4 - 8	8" round bowl -	$ 8 - 15
fruit cup -	$6 - 12		

───────────────────── *Alara* ─────────────────────

Alara, from the Latin "alaris" meaning "wings", was made by Mt. Clemens and was sold to the Stetson Pottery Company who would decorate blanks with decal treatments. Here the line is found in the same solid colors used for Mt. Clemens' Petal: maroon, green, blue and yellow. Though both companies used this shape, it is safe to assume that in the colored glazes this is a Mt. Clemens product only.

Of the pieces I've seen, none have been marked. Since undecorated blanks were sold to Stetson, it may have been standard practice not to mark any of the Alara pieces.

You will find far less solid colored Alara than the other Mt. Clemens line, Petal.

Plates in 9", 7" and 6" sizes.

Cups and saucers in the four standard colors.

Fruit cups

Creamer in maroon.

ALARA VALUES: This line is not easily found and not well known. Because there is little interest at this time, values are low.

9" plate -	$6-8	creamer -	$6-8
7" plate -	$4-6	sugar -	$8-10
6" plate -	$3-5	platter -	$8-10
cup -	$4-6	saucer -	$1-2

Platter in yellow.

—— *Lines by Other Potteries: Zephyr* ——

Produced by the Cronin China Company of Minerva, Ohio in the late 1930s, Zephyr is one of the more unusual color dinnerware lines. The ring pattern is Fiesta except there is a lack of center rings on flat pieces. The cups have an angular handle like Harlequin's and the shakers are designed with holes on the side. The color assortment for this line is red, maroon, medium blue, green, turquoise, yellow, beige and cobalt.

Most of the time, the Zephyr shape was used as the basis for decals. It is light weight so damage occurs easily, and virtually every piece will be crazed. The solid colored Zephyr was sold through Hamilton Ross. A service for eight could be ordered, complete with Catalin flatware and glasses with swizzle sticks for $14.95. The dinnerware ensemble was promoted as, "Hollywood Colors." Each of the eight colors were given special names which referred to various parts of the Hollywood/Los Angeles area:

Wilshire Yellow -	yellow	Pico Turquoise -	turquoise
Avalon Blue -	cobalt	Catalina Green -	green
Sycamore Brown -	beige	Beverly Blue -	medium blue
La Brea Burgundy -	maroon	Pasadena Rose -	red

Pink and Gray are also found.

Zephyr plates: 9" in turquoise and yellow, 7" in cobalt.

Zephyr plates: 9" in turquoise and yellow, 7" in cobalt.

This is the smaller of two round platters found in the Zephyr line. It measures 11 1/4" from one extreme to the other with its "wings" flowing in a counterclockwise direction. The larger round platter is 13 1/4" and has wings running in a clockwise direction. Almost every platter found is green, though a few have been found in maroon.

Zephyr cups and saucers in yellow, cobalt, green, beige, red and medium blue. The cups are commonly misidentified as Harlequin.

Zephyr fruit cups in yellow, green and red.

The sugar and creamer shown are restyled versions. The originals are shaped very much like the teacups with conical bodies and angular handles. These restyled versions have much more curvature to both their bodies and handles than their predecessors.

Shown both in red: left-restyled sugar, right-the original sugar. Notice how the body and angular handles of the original resemble the Zephyr teacups. Original style sugars and creamers, which are also angular in nature, are harder to find than the restyled versions.

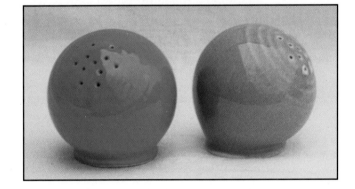

Zephyr shakers. These shakers are often identified as being Fiesta.

Cronin produced several kitchen ware items commonly found with decal treatments. Once in a while, an item will appear in a solid color glaze.

Cronin also used BAKE OVEN in an oval as a marking for several of their kitchen ware items. Shown in red is the base of the Zephyr Kitchenware drip jar. It has a Bake Oven marking.

These pie plates, found most often in light green and cobalt, are constantly being confused for Harlequin. The ring pattern is almost identical, but this plate belongs to the Zephyr Kitchenware line. The pie plates, like virtually every other piece of Zephyr, are unmarked.

VALUE: pie plate - $20

ZEPHYR VALUES: any color:

9" plates -	$8-10	coupe soup -	$6-8
7" plates -	$5-7	round serving bowl -	$12-15
11" platter -	$12-15	shakers, per pair -	$8-10
13" platter -	$15-18	covered sugar, original -	$18-20
cup -	$6-8	covered sugar, restyled -	$12-15
saucer -	$2-3	creamer, original -	$16-18
fruit cup -	$5-7	creamer, restyled -	$10-12

Georgette

Georgette, made by W.S. George, is commonly known as Petal or Petalware. Be aware it is not the same as Petal made by Mt. Clemens Pottery Company. W.S. George made several colored dinnerware lines including Rainbow (similar to HLC's Tango), Petitpoint Rainbow, Elmhurst, Basketweave and Bolero, but it is Georgette which is the most readily found. The easiest colors found are light green, medium blue, rose, gray, yellow, and pink. Colors which are little more difficult to find are aqua, chartreuse, forest green, and maroon.

The basic shapes for Georgette are round with panels (or petals) extending outward. Finials and handles are rather simply designed.

Georgette is gaining in popularity. Prices are starting to rise dramatically for this line and it is easy to see why. It is substantial ware able to take use and seldom chips or cracks. The colors are softer than the bold colors of the 30s and early 40s and generally are clean and even with no crazing. All of the items are somewhat easy to find; the only exception would have to be the casserole. Sugars are often found without lids and incorrectly labeled, "cream soup cups" by dealers.

Georgette: 9½" plate in rose, 7¾" coupe soup bowl in medium blue, 5½" fruit cup in gray.

VALUES: 9½" plate - $8-10
coupe soup - $10-12
fruit cup - $5-7

W.S. George used a generic shape of shakers for many of their lines. Shown in chartreuse, these can be found in an assortment of decal treatments.

VALUES: $12-18 a pair

Here are three shades of red found in Georgette. In the back is a soup bowl in maroon, and in the front is a creamer in pink. In between is rose.

VALUES: coupe soup - $10-12
fruit cup - $5-7
creamer - $10-12

7 3/4" Soup bowls
VALUES: $10-12

Somewhat hard to find sauce boat in green.
VALUES: $15-18

Covered sugar in chartreuse with yellow 5" fruit cup. There is a large number of sugars being found without lids. Sometimes they are incorrectly labeled as cream soups.

VALUES: covd sugar - $20-25
open sugar - $10-12
fruit cup - $5-7

Platter in rose and oval baker in gray.

VALUES: platter - $10-12
baker - $6-9
Not shown: round serving bowl - $10-12
36s bowl - $8-10

Cup and saucer in pink.

VALUES: cup - $8-10
saucer - $3-4

Sevilla Pottery

Anyone who has walked into an antiques and collectibles shop has seen a piece of Sevilla! Sevilla was a trademark used by Cronin China. Its marking can be found on the larger items such as mixing bowls, casseroles and cookie jars. Once in a while a "Bake Oven" marking is found on these items; another Cronin mark.

All too often, Sevilla items are confused for Fiesta and Harlequin. Juice sets, mixing bowls, ball jugs and novelty creamers are commonly and incorrectly labeled as Fiesta. Shown in this section are just a few of the many Sevilla items which were produced.

Most Sevilla pieces are unmarked. Shown is the underside of a cobalt ball jug. It has a completely dry underside with a well defined seam line. It seems that the earlier Sevilla items had this type of bottom. Later pieces have a dry foot ring which has an irregular shape as compared to the dry foot rings of larger potteries. Many of the small items with the dry foot ring were unmarked but some can be found with a raised

"U.S.A." Larger items such as the mixing bowls and various covered jars are marked with a raised "Sevilla, U.S.A." in script.

Colors include green, medium blue, cobalt blue, yellow, maroon, pink and red. The Fiesta type red is generally applied over a pre-existing ivory or white glaze. The red cold paint color has a matte finish and tends to flake off easily. Sometimes when the item has a completely dry underside, you can see the over spray of the red coloring.

You will find various sizes of mixing bowls in green, yellow, maroon and medium blue. They are fairly common, but more often than not, they are found with heavy crazing. The mixing bowls have a raised "Sevilla" script marking.

Sevilla covered sugar and creamer in maroon. These have three curved lines on either side. The triple line design can also be found on coffeepots and teapots.

Shown in the red-on-white glaze, this Sevilla coffeepot was originally sold with a metal drip-o-lator.

Swan planters. The blue one was sent to me by a collector who thought it was Sevilla because of its color, dry underside, and visible seam line. Later it was confirmed when the second swan planter was found with the distinctive red-on-white color application.

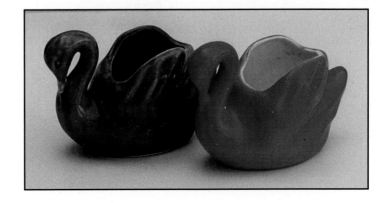

Cronin large cookie jar. This is one of the few items which is marked Sevilla in script. It has a ring configuration in the middle which matches the mixing bowls.

This little cup, probably a condiment piece for mustard or jam, has a fry foot ring and is unmarked. The leafy design matches a corresponding creamer and sugar.

Sevilla leafy cream and sugar. These are easy to find in the red glaze.

Sevilla juice set. It is easy to see why many people confuse this set with Fiesta. The tumblers are slightly taller than Fiesta's and they have a flare to the openings. Note the cobalt tumbler: it has a very thick and irregular dry ring. Fiesta's tumblers have very clean and regular dry rings so this should help in determining which is which. Also notice the red-on-white tumbler in the middle: a distinctive Sevilla color.

These tumblers have been found in the colors shown as well as medium blue and maroon.

The pitcher has a completely dry underside.

A pair of Sevilla novelty vases.
These stand 4 1/2".

Sevilla disc pitchers in maroon and green.

Sevilla elephant planters. According to a G. Sommors Wholesale catalog from 1940, the Sevilla elephant planters were made in yellow and white only. They stand almost 3 1/2" tall and are 5" long.

This Sevilla flowerpot stands 31/4" tall and has an opening diameter of 31/2". There is a repeated leaf design along the side of the planter, but the glaze is so heavy, it barely shows. These little flower pots can sometimes be found with an attached saucer.

Novelty pitchers. To the left is the common style in yellow. On the right is a pitcher with a ruffled opening in red. Both styles stand only 21/2" tall.

Sevilla novelity pitchers; cobalt, red, white, maroon.

Footed Sevilla sugar and creamer. The sugar doesn't come with a lid. I recently saw a sugar in green in a shop that was incorrectly labeled as "Rare Lu-Ray sugar." The asking price was $30!!

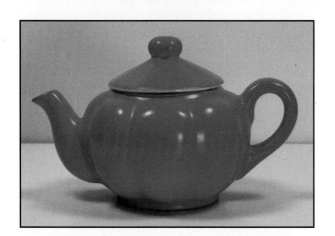

This Sevilla teapot is hard to find in the red-on-white glaze. More often than not, it is found in pink and green.

Two Sevilla candidates: Irish setter and lamb planter. These two planters have been found in medium blue (as shown) pink, yellow and green. More than likely these are the work of Sevilla since the colors are right and they have the characteristic undersides of dry foot/seam line. The lamb comes in at least two sizes.

Sevilla heart vases. The larger vase stands 3 1/4”; the small version, 2 1/4”.

Shown in cobalt is the ball Sevilla sugar. The smaller handle in this example is filled in, but you can find versions with an open small handle. The red ball creamer on the right is the most common piece of Sevilla found.

This covered casserole has the Cronin Sevilla script marking.

Sevilla teapot. These can be found with and without metal drip-o-lators. Green teapots are common and almost always mistaken for Fiesta.

The Sevilla mini-disc pitcher. Look for the completely dry underside of this little pitcher. These have been found in green, cobalt, yellow and red. Like the teapot, tumblers and large disc pitcher, the mini disc pitcher is often mislabeled, "Fiesta."

Sevilla shakers. The moon-shaped shakers on the left belong to a range set. Each stands on either side of a cylindrical drip jar. The smaller shakers are rather common and match the ball jug and creamer. Notice the rib design in the filled space in the green shaker. Sometimes the glaze is so heavy on Sevilla items that details such as these are hard to see.

The white duck planter is a Sevilla product. The other duck is slightly larger than the white version and may or may not have been made at Cronin.

Though there are no records to confirm this, the items shown have all the characteristics of being Sevilla products. They are all in the red-on-white glaze and have completely dry undersides.

The sugar and creamer have a band of rings towards the openings which are similar to the teapot. Carafe lids are rather thin and don't fit the base properly.

Sevilla was widely distributed and is very easy to find anywhere in the country today. There isn't much demand for Sevilla, so prices for any piece should be low.

As for small novelty items such as planters, tumblers, shakers, creamers, sugars, ewers and vases, you shouldn't have to pay any more than $10.00.

Larger items such as mixing bowls, large ball jugs, disc pitchers, teapots, coffeepots, casseroles and carafes should be no more than $20.00.

Keep in mind that these pieces are easy to find, so if you come across something that seems overpriced, have some patience; more than likely it will show up somewhere else with a lower price tag. Also remember that it may be hard to find items without some level of crazing.

What has been presented in this section is just a small sample of Sevilla pottery. If you decide to collect this ware, then this is the time. Since little is known about it and since there is no demand, prices should remain low.

Zephyr Shape: Romany and Rancho

There are two lines of solid colored dinnerware that come from the same general shape. The shape is Zephyr (not to be confused with Zephyr by Cronin China) which was produced by the French-Saxon China Co. in the late 1930s. Zephyr, like almost every other line produced by small potteries, pulled double duty as being made in both solid colors and with decals. It has a scalloped section that is repeated four times around flat ware and angular handles and finials on the hollow items.

The first line is called Romany or Grenada. It comes in bold 30s Fiesta-like colors and were listed in one vintage advertisement as: Nile Green, Tangerine, Navy Blue and Maize (yellow).

The later line is called Rancho. The colors for this line are typical late 40s early 50s colors that include gray, chartreuse, maroon, and dark green.

Since the shapes are basically the same, collectors tend to mix Romany and Rancho together. The later Rancho items are a little thicker and heavier. Some hollow ware items also have slight variation in shape and lighter colors seem to craze more than others. Chartreuse from Rancho and yellow from Romany almost always have some level of crazing while gray and dark green are the best with clean and even glazes.

9 1/8" Rancho plates in chartreuse and maroon.
6" Romany plate in red.

From left to right: Gray Rancho cup and saucer, back center - yellow Romany cup and saucer, far right - dark green Rancho cup and saucer.

Romany covered sugar in red and creamer in turquoise.

Shakers in maroon and yellow. These can be easily identified by the trademark "cow lick" tops.

These tall shakers made by French-Saxon are commonly associated with Romany. It is surprising though, considering their overall shape is dissimilar to the rest of the pieces in the Zephyr line.

Left: red Romany teacup. Right: Rancho teacup in dark green. Notice the wider and slightly lower body of the green cup. The later Rancho teacups will also have thicker walls.

To evaluate Romany and Ranchero, use the prices given for Knowles' Yorktown and Deanna lines.

Camwood Ivory

Introduced in the 1930s by the Universal Pottery Co., Camwood Ivory in solid colors is not easily found. Shown are four glazes which are the most common, but you may find others. Camwood Ivory was sold as "Sunny Lane" and came in Periwinkle blue, Coca tan, Jade green, and Jonquil yellow.

Four 6 1/4" plates in Jade, Jonquil, Periwinkle and tan.

Covered casserole in Jonquil.

Tab handled serving platter in tan.

Cups and saucers.

Dinner plates.

Camwood Ivory is somewhat extensive with 29 items. Other than being found with decal treatments, this line can be found in an ivory or white glaze decorated simply with gold or red trim. This line is rare in solid colors so it is uncertain how many of the 29 standard items were given colored glazes. Remember, for lesser known lines such as Camwood Ivory, low demand equals low prices. Just because it is hard to find doesn't mean the cost should be higher than normal. Obtaining a complete set of this line in solid colors piece by piece would be a feat indeed.

VALUES: any color

91/4" plate - $10	cassrole - $15
61/4" plate - $6	lug serving platter - $12
51/4" Fruit cup - $5	tea cup - $7
77/8" Soup bowl - $8	saucer - $1.50
creamer - $8	36s bowl - $6
sugar - $10	shakers, pair - $10

The name of this shape is "Colonial White." It was produced by Homer Laughlin during the 1970s and can be found with in a white body with decal treatments and in typical 70s colors such as brown, gold and olive green.

The red sauceboat must have been dipped around the time of Fiesta Ironstone. The 7" plate was done much later since it is in the reissue green of Harlequin. Green, yellow and brown pieces are somewhat easy to find.

Coronet

Homer Laughlin collectors should be able to recognize this shape. It is Coronet which was made in solid colors before Fiesta, Harlequin and the other HLC colored dinnerware lines. In 1935, it was offered in ming yellow, old ivory and sea green. This shape has a set of panels with a thin wreath of flowers.

When the Coronet shape is found, it is generally with decal treatments. The solid colors are much more desirable since they bring out the heavy sculpting of the ware.

Large platter in ming yellow. Coronet is a circular shape so the platters seem a little out of place with their double "fish tail" tabs.

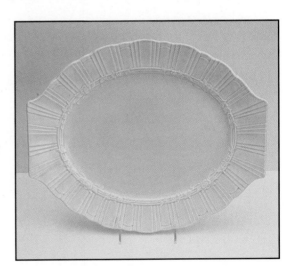

A place setting in sea green.

Marigold

This is an example of HLC's Marigold in Fiesta's light green glaze. Small pieces such as soup bowls, fruit cups, cups and saucers turn up every once in a while. Of the pieces I've seen, all have a 1937 backstamp and many believe small Marigold items in light green were promotional items like Carnival and the small Oven Serve pieces. However, this is no documentation to support this.

Mixing Bowl

This mixing bowl is one of a set that can be found in various glazes such as red, cobalt, green and yellow. Many have speculated that this is not only the work of HLC but a piece of Fiesta. The ring spacing and placement is right, but I don't believe it is in fact Fiesta. There is no mention of it in the modeling log that I can find, and the glaze has a matte finish – not at all like Fiesta's red glaze. Most HLC items in red have a slight gloss to them.

These two bowls are from Hall China's Five Band line. They are very similar in size and overall shape to the unknown mixing bowl often confused for Fiesta. The unknown mixing bowl bears more resemblance to these Hall China bowls than to any HLC piece.

King Edward & F.E. Willard Plates

These two plates have been the subject of various online debates over the past few years. The brown 10" plate reads, "Commemorating the coronation of His Majesty King Edward VIII, May Twelfth Nineteen Hundred and Thirty Seven." This plate has been found in maroon, light green, mauve blue and ivory.

The King Edward plates have an interesting story behind them. In 1937 when King Edward abdicated the throne, King Edward pieces such as plates, mugs and other wares declaring his ascension and coronation became sought after. According to a 1938 copy of *China, Glass and Lamps* Salem China took advantage of this by creating this coronation plate *after* Edward abdicated.

Shown in medium blue is the "Frances E. Willard Centenary, 1839-1939" plate. This plate shows much better workmanship than the King Edward plate. F.E. Willard was an educator and president of Evanston College for Ladies in 1871, president of National Woman's Temperance Union in 1879, and founder of World's Christian Temperance Union, 1883. The Willard plate has the exact same dimension, weight and feel of the King Edward plate.

VALUES: Entire plate, any color - $30-40

These two bowls, made by Salem China, are no doubt specialty salad bowls not belonging

Salem China Salad Bowls

to any particular line. The example on the left has a floral decal treatment in the bottom with a pink was trim. These can be found with blue, green and yellow trims. The salad bowl on the right is unusual because it is glazed in a solid color.

VALUES: with trim and decal - $10
in solid color - $15

Shell Plate

Steve Sfakis shares this unusual 10" plate that was found in the Newell-East Liverpool area. He speculated it was an HLC product based on the color and the "feel" of the plate. He was right! The shell plate appears in the modeling log as #1203 and being modeled by "R + K" (Rhead and Kraft??) in 1939. The description is given simply as, Plate, Shell, 10$1/2$".

There were other shell plates mentioned in the log book. Number 1123, is the 7" equivalent to the 10$1/2$" design. Numbers 1127 and 1128 were also 7" shell plates with a variation to the shell design and actual depth of the plate. All three of the 7" shell plates were modeled by Berrisford in September of 1938.

Trials and experimentals are always great finds so it is difficult to price something like the shell plate. There are different groups of collectors: some only want that which is Genuine Fiesta while others will take anything unusual that HLC did as experiments that can be found in Fiesta glazes.

Kraft Leaf Saucer

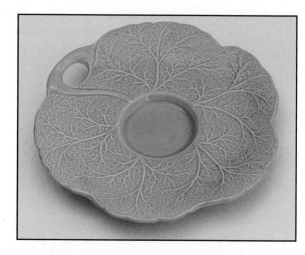

Leaf saucers were made by Homer Laughlin for the Kraft Cheese Co. It was modeled in March of 1938 and is listed as having a diameter of 7". Shown along side the saucer are two Swanky Swigs. These small glass containers came in a wide variety of colors and floral patterns. Kraft would use these swigs as containers for cheese. They were sealed with a metal lid which generally had an advertisement for some other Kraft food. One of the swigs shown in the picture has an original lid advertising the leaf saucer. It reads:

THIS SMART SNACK PLATE FOR ONLY 25¢ AND TWO JAR LABELS FROM KRAFT CHEESE SPREADS. "FIESTA" COLORS: RED OR GREEN.

Then in smaller letters it has, off to the side: Snack Plate Made by the makers of "FIESTA" Ware. The leaf saucer has been found in both red and light green and so far, none have been found with any marking.

VALUES: Kraft leaf saucer (red or green) - $75-85
original metal lid showing ad for saucer - $30

Betty Crocker Bowls

These Betty Crocker bowls were made by Homer Laughlin around 1940. They have been found in both Harlequin and Fiesta yellow as well as turquoise. One collector reports one in red, but it has not been confirmed. Once in a while the "Betty Bowl" is found with a metal holder which can fold when not in use.

VALUES: $10-15

There are several variations of backstamps but they all read the same: Betty Crocker, (Trade Mark) GMI. The "GMI" stands for General Mills Industries.

Red Wing and Gladding McBean also made these bowls. The Homer Laughlin Betty Crocker bowl has a diameter of 8½" and stands 2¾" tall.

When I was on a buying trip in February of 1999, I found four of these bowls in turquoise on the day. Needless to say they are not terribly hard to find. I have noticed that they are usually heavily worn so watch for nicks along the rim as well as utensil marks along the inner walls.

Ornate Salad Plates

The ornate salad plate was made by Homer Laughlin. It is a relatively new piece glazed in cobalt from new Fiesta. A group of these were purchased at the outlet a few years ago – all in cobalt and all unmarked. The box was simply labeled, Ornate Salad Plate, Fiesta Cobalt.

VALUES: $25+

The red dinner plate is Williamsburg by Knowles. Many times this pattern is found with decal treatments, but some flat pieces are turning up in solid colors.

The smaller plate is called Old Rose and is from an extensive line of dinnerware from the early 30s. This is a line similar to HLC's Coronet in that it comes from the days before mixing and matching solid colors.

Georgex Teapots

This teapot was made by the W.S. George Company. It is from the Ranchero line – a pattern used for decal treatments. In the very late 30s, W.S. George offered the Ranchero teapots in four glazes: blue, pink, yellow and turquoise. The teapots were sold under the name, "Georgex."

The following is from an advertisement found in *China Glass and Lamps,* December 1939.

"This new W.S. George item is made of a new material developed at this pottery – Georgex – extra hard and heat resisting guaranteed against crazing and with ordinary care will not chip or crack. Now pour boiling hot water over the tea right into this beautiful GEORGEX teapot . . ."

The ad also states: **"Hard to break!"** "Remove lid and tap it sharply against the side of the teapot – will not break, chip or crack."

VALUES: any color - $25-30

About a month into working on this book, I was in a local Wal-Mart and found this set of dishes called Mix-N-Match made by Gibson China. The ring pattern on the edge is similar to Fiesta and many of the colors can be found in the new Fiesta line. I toyed with the idea that I should at least mention the existence of this line since it could be easily confused with Fiesta. About two weeks later, I saw an unmarked turquoise plate from Mix-N-Match which was listed as "Fiesta" on eBay and selling for over $10.00. So, because of that auction, here is the Mix-N-Match line!

Colors include: periwinkle, turquoise, yellow, rose, persimmon, jade and lavender. Most of these items will have a Gibson backstamp, but not all. This line is very limited with only the most common of pieces: 10" plate, 7" plate, cereal bowl, and mug. Most recently a cookie jar, platter, shakers and a serving bowl were added. This line even has a set of accessories similar to Fiesta's which include flatware and drinking glasses. Gibson also makes pedestal and jumbo mugs, but they are plain without decoration.

Two other look-alike lines have recently come out: one similar to Mix-N-Match but called: Match-N-Mix! The other is Petal and has the look of Fiesta in almost every way except each piece has a molded flower in the center. The colors for Petal are very similar to both old and new Fiesta shades.

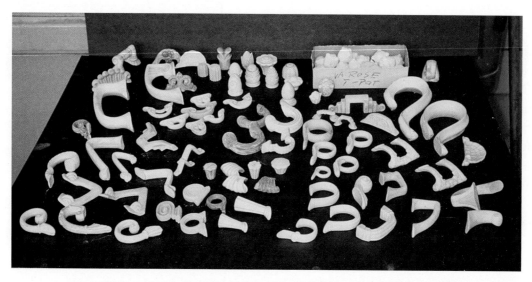

HLC Finial and handle models from the 20s, 30s, 40s, and 50s.

Close up showing the various Fiesta and Harlequin models.
Notice the various trials of Fiesta teacup handles.

HOMER LAUGHLIN (HLC):
Full name: The Homer Laughlin China Company
Dates of operation: 1871-present
Location: East Liverpool, Ohio 1971-1929
                    Newell, West Virginia 1904-present
Owners: Homer Laughlin
            Shakespeare Laughlin (original co-owner and brother to Homer)

TAYLOR SMITH AND TAYLOR (TS & T or TST):
Full name: Taylor, Smith & Taylor Company (originally Taylor, Smith & Lee.)
Dates of operation: 1871-present
Location: Chester, West Virginia
Original Owners: John Taylor
                            Charles Smith
                            William Smith
                            Joseph Lee
Notes: - Lee left the company after the first year. Consequently the name was changed
            from Taylor, Smith and Lee to Taylor, Smith and Taylor.
        - Anchor Hocking purchased TS & T in 1972 and kept it open until 1981
        - The plant still stands in Chester, West Virginia, but it is in terrible shape.

        Years of neglect and bad snow storms have caused large sections of the roof to cave in.

KNOWLES:
Full name: Edwin M. Knowles China Company
Dates of operation: 1900-1963
Location: Chester, West Virginia
                    Newell, West Virginia
Original Owners: Edwin M. Knowles
Notes: - The original Chester plant was sold to Harker Pottery, also located in Chester, in 1931.

W.S. GEORGE:
Full name: W.S. George Pottery Company
Dates of operation: 1900-1955
Location: East Palestine, Ohio
Original Owners: W.S. George
Notes: - also had plants in Canonsburg and Kittaning, Pennsylvania.

CRONIN:
Full name: Cronin China Company
Dates of operation: 1934-1956
Location: Minerva, Ohio
Original Owners: Dan Cronin
Notes: - Cronin bought the already existing plant in Minerva called The Owen China
            Company which began operating in 1900.

MT. CLEMENS (MCPCO):
Full name: Mt. Clemens Pottery Company
Dates of operation: 1915-1987
Location: Mt. Clemens, Michigan
Owners: S.S. Kresge
Notes: - S.S. Kresge is known today as K-Mart.
   - Technically, Mt. Clemens was a subsidiary of Kresge. This gave Kresge the great
      advantage over other retailers since they had a firm supply of dinnerware to sell.

Appendix II: Bibliography

Cunningham, Jo. *Homer Laughlin A Giant Among Dishes.* Schiffer Publishing, 1998.

Cunningham, Jo. *The Collector's Encyclopedia of American Dinnerware.* Collector Books, 1982.

Duke, Harvey. *The Official Price Guide to Pottery and Porcelain, 8th Edition.*
      Collector Books, 1995.

Huxford, Sharon and Bob. *The Collector's Encyclopedia of Fiesta, 7th Edition.*
      Collector Books, 1995.

Meehan, Bill and Kathy. *Collector's Guide to Lu-Ray Pastels.*   Collector Books, 1995.

Lehner Lois. *Lehner's Encyclopedia of U.S. Marks on Pottery, Porcelain & Clay.*
      Collector Books, 1988.

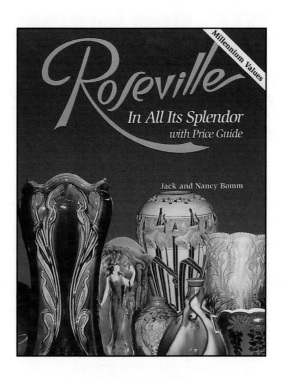

Item #1112
Only $39.95 + $3.00 Shipping
UPDATED PRICE GUIDE - YEAR 2000

Roseville Pottery is one of the largest and most extensive pottery lines in today's antique and collectible market. You can go to any show, antique mall or antique shop and find a piece of Roseville. Do not be left behind in the discovery of pieces of Roseville that have never been identified in any book until now. Many trade publication's surveys say that Roseville is the #1 collectible on the market. This is the most complete reference book on Roseville pottery to date. You would have to buy all the other Roseville books on the market, plus some of the general guides, and you would still not be able to equal the volume of Roseville pottery in "*Roseville In All Its Splendor*", which could cost you over $160. There are many new and unknown patterns listed and pictured. Patterns only touched on by other books is described and shown. There are around 500 Roseville Pottery Co. plates showing all of the known patterns made. Jack and Nancy Bomm have researched this for over 5 years and the current leaders of the Rosevilles of the Past Collectors Club, which is the only collectors club just for Roseville pottery.

The book is 8½" x 11", Hardbound, and over 400 pages, full color, with price guide.

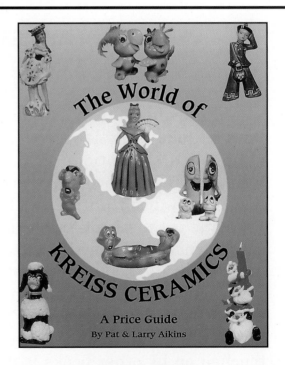